RICHARD MICHAEL DELGADO

TRUMP
PROVERBS
A MAN AFTER GODS OWN HEART

Ordering Information:

Books to Life Marketing

Books to Life Marketing Ltd
128 City Road, London, EC1V 2NX, UK

Printed in the United States of America

BOOK ITINERARY

INTRODUCTION TO TRUMP PROVERBS

What does a man believe in when his Nation is Failing, and his Country is being destroyed by Communist and Atheist and those who hate America?

He first takes what **He believes in,** and places this Baton in his Hand, and Runs the **Marathon of Victory.**

And with that said, he Challenges and takes Captive the wrongs of pain and destruction and deception and locks them up, and places them in a cave and buries them, and leaves them they're for Eternity.

This Character of Leadership and Passion for what is Good and Excellent for the land called America, is what our Forefathers Instilled in their Writings; and passed them unto us to become a Great and Mighty nation called,

The United States of America.

And what this Man Has Done, is more far reaching then any President has done in History. And You may ask the question: 'How so?', well your answer is very simple.

"He Kept Every Promise He made!"

May We the People pay good attention to what One Man has accomplished in History, for because of His Performance!

……… the World Hates Him! ………

His name is … President Donald Trump!

OUR FOREFATHERS BELIEF SYSTEM

In order to have a Belief System, you have to be Educated, and someone must educate you and be schooled by a Teacher of Knowledge.

What do you think? ... were they ignorant and stupid?

Our Forefathers, Studied the Bible and the Classics and the basics of English, Arithmetic, History, Geometry, and yes; including crayons to draw pictures of their dreams and things to come.

For they were Homeschooled, such as the one room schoolhouse, is where they got their education.

They all knew what country living was all about and they lived it to the fullest. They worked hard and good to succeed in what they all **Believed In.**

So, the question you must ask yourself?

What Education are you living by, and what Information has lodge inside your Heart. Because what Lives and Reigns in your Heart, Determines the Life you will live.

If Evil is present in your Heart, Evil you will do!

If Good is present in your Heart, Good you will do!

You have only **One Choice** to live by, to die in righteous standing with a great and wonderful legacy.

Or…

Your Choice will lead you, to a Dishonorable life and you will die without Honors.

Our Founding Fathers, all died with Honors and Majestic Praise, for they all created the wonderful History of America.

And by their simple dedication and desire to be Free, and Prosperous and to have the Freedom of Worship; they all passed away knowing their Future was an Eternal one.

Are You willing to continue their Legacy?

WHAT IS THIS BOOK ABOUT

The contents of this Proverbial Book are to explain in simple terms, what is the Mind of a Man who seeks to do good for the people and to deliver His Promises from His Oath of Office.

The True Passion of a Champion is one who determines beforehand what He will have to endure and overcome and embrace that struggle, and carry it into the Promise Land.

This Remarkable Talent and Skill and Ingenuity and Wisdom and Comprehensive Knowledge that this Man has, was formed by the negative pressures to destroy Him; and with that said, His Dignity of Discretion and His Diplomatic Excellence, is what He has offered and presented to our American Citizens, the People of the United States of America!

And because of His **Passion Of Excellence** for You and Us, we stand in awe of His Wonderful Resilience of Strength and Honor, which comes Directly from His Heart.

And in His Heart, He has placed the Creator of the Universe to Reside their Forever, to give Him Counsel and Advise to lead a country into the Spirit of Righteousness, where God will Bless us with His Riches and Glory.

Therefore, saving us and protecting us from our foreign enemies, who seek to destroy our Country, which still Stands upon a Hill!

Lets Us All follow His Steps, and Build for us a Better America, a Dream our Founding Fathers had from the very beginning of time; that We the People would benefit for ourselves and for our children, …. **Forever!**

A TRUE AMERICAN IN BATTLE

When a Man comes before the World, And discovers it is in trouble…….

He then steps into the Chaos of Mud and Slime, and searches for the best solution possible…

And once he does, **He then seeks** the guidance and discretion of the Almighty God, the God of the Universe, who has placed His Signature upon our hearts.

And then ask for His Dignity, Justice, and Integrity and **Stands** upon the Forefathers Directives………!

The Constitution of the United States

And the

Declaration of Independence

A MAN AFTER GOD'S OWN HEART

I Believe, that President Donald Trump is a Man of his Word and He is determined to be an **Honorable Man of Integrity**.

And because of that, I as the Author have taken the Freedom to show the World, ... that the Power of Integrity does Shine in His Heart!

For our History reveals the Hymns that make the Liberty Bell sing for Freedom. Our Forefathers are Great People, **and we are** descendants of their Greatness!

They put forth their effort, to do only one thing in life, to make America Great continuously, from day to day to everyday and in every way.

Are You That Kind of Patriot!

Do You have a Heart, that seeks after Gods Principles that has made our Country Superior and Great, from its beginning? For without this Passion to run the Race of Excellence, then we will cease to be a Great Nation.

We need each other, from both sides of the isle of Government, and we need to be kind to one another; ... a Biblical Principle that has made us Great!

As King David was Chosen by God to be made a King over Israel, so today, **I Believe** God has Chosen President Donald Trump to be our President of America.

Why may you ask? Because He President Donald Trump, Values the Core Essence of Gods Will for America.

That America would Stand on the Promises God has given to us as a Nation; … and what would those Promises be?

Jeremiah 29:11–12

> "For I know the thoughts that I think toward you, says the LORD, thoughts of peace and not of evil, to give you a future and a hope. Then you will call upon Me and go and pray to Me, and I will listen to you."

This is what President Donald Trump wants for America, he wants America to be under the Shadow of His Wings, where Gods Blessings and Prosperity and Freedom of Hope are they're as a Treasure for the American People, of the United States of America.

TRUMP PROVERBS

CHAPTER 1

I Believe

that every American should have a Chance.

I Believe

that God Almighty has already planned your life.

I Believe

fairness is what we need, in dealing with each other.

I Believe

a Sacred Promise in Office, is what every official is to keep.

I Believe

every American has a positive destiny.

I Believe

in honoring my country called: America!

I Believe

my Family is the most important thing on earth.

I Believe

in the Constitution of the United States, because it works for the Good of the People!

I Believe

in the System of Justice, put forth by our Founding Fathers.

I Believe

that our Country America, deserves a people of good and great character.

I Believe

every emigrant who wants Freedom, deserves to live here in America.

I Believe

in the Almighty who created the heavens and the earth, and that includes you too.

I Believe

that Marriage is the Cornerstone of our American Society.

I Believe

that every living American who wants True Justice, should and must live Justly.

I Believe

in the American Dream, and so I want each American to Desire the same.

I Believe

that the love between a Father and a Mother is sacred and honorable, for that love itself produces a true garden of red and white roses.

I Believe

that anyone who holds an Official Office in Government should be blameless and clear of any misdoings; that way the people of America can vote the right person in.

I Believe

that Honesty is the Best policy when negotiating what is Right and what is Wrong; especially when Justice is on the table of affairs.

I Believe

that the currency we now have, with the words imprinted: "In God We Trust" were their placed by President Dwight Eisenhower, to show the Faith of our Nation and Founded by Christian Principles.

I Believe

that God only has the Power to Protect America from foreign enemies, and including Protecting our Families from political unrest.

I Believe

righteous rules with good intention, protect our sovereign land into prosperity and peace.

I Believe

the Leadership from our Forefathers came with the ability to trust God and trust each other; into having a Great Nation.

I Believe

dignity is a word that reveals the heart of every man, from humility: onto a stepping stone, from respect: onto a pathway, from honor: onto a bridge of hope.

I Believe

being Married to Mrs. Melania Trump, at times I feel unworthy, for She is a Honorable Lady filled with a Beautiful Treasure of Royal Diplomacy;

for She Sparkles when She Smiles and when She Speaks, the Angels gather around Her for joy. For Her Heart is Held in the Hand of the Almighty, and because of that; She is a Woman of Magnificent Honor and Character, and She Exemplifies Gods Attributes, as a Lady of Grace.

I Believe

That life is very short, and it only consist of what we do, in return favor for our country and Forefathers; and that includes our Moms and Dads and Brothers and Sisters; **may we make them proud**.

TRUMP PROVERBS

CHAPTER 2

I Believe

that the word for Constitution, means exactly what it means, "The basic principles and laws of our Nation, to keep it safe and secure under God Almighty." so if you decide to destroy these Transcripts from Heaven, … then what will you replace it with?

I Believe

you and I have a Duty to Perform before our days are completed, from good service and a plausible Excellent Servitude to our Nation; reason is, our Children will Follow after, and become our Workmanship of Art …. Our Example!

I Believe

in having a strong Military Presence, to Protect our Country from harm in arms way, it is fully and necessarily important for World Peace. Here is a quote from President George Washington: "To be prepared for war is one of the most effectual means of preserving peace."

I Believe

that the Gay Movement **with all of their ideology**, needs our Help to survive, yes, they want to promote their lifestyle to our children and indoctrinate them in School **to become like them;** but, if we all became like them, … what would our Nation be like or look like? And what could we accomplish with that? We should Pray for Peace in their Heart, that they would be comforted.

I Believe

that Helping One Another is a vital chemistry of life in itself, as a Child needs a Mothers Love for comfort, and a Teenager needs patience to learn the way, and a Grand Parent needs assistance to continue before they pass; we look at our current condition now, … we have over 20 Million youths **who do not have a Father**, and they desperately Need One. So, where are the **Fathers** of our Land?

I Believe

that Justice must be served Properly and Ethically, and that Honesty and Integrity must be in the Heart of all the people; especially in the Department of Justice, where accountability is the Scale of Justice.

I Believe

that Divorce is brutal with a deadly force, for it crushes the soul and the heart of a person. We were not designed for this act, but it does happen; and when it occurs, we should peacefully and humbly ask for forgiveness; and help each other along the way With Honor and Respect, into their next chapter of life.

I Believe

justice prevails in life and in our History of this Nation, and it will always be Victorious and Truthful in its Divine Endeavors; it is when we take into account that God has established this Measure of Balance, a Scale for Humanity, to exist and live in Peace.

I Believe

justice in America Serves its Jurisprudence, as we exercise our fundamental rights and liberties within the Framers of the Constitution of the United States and the Declaration of Independence; for they understood by its Divine Meaning, that we should study with the essence of integrity and examine with the spirit of dignity, and judge with diplomatic righteousness; to bring forth a Judgement of Fairness, for this is why America exist today. It is a Great Nation Because of This Practice.!

I Believe

our Nation is in need of Healing, from Deception and Assault upon the American people, for the **'Media'** has no compassion for truth, and neither do they have mercy, for Pristine Justice; **all they care about** is having power over the simple minds of the People of the United States of America.

I Believe

in Fair Justice, under the Constitution of the United States, where all people are examined with the peaceful Scales of Integrity, and with the essence of American Favoritism; for we have a Heavenly Compass that Navigates Divinely towards the North Star. This is where Justice originated.

I Believe

that Thomas Jefferson's view of the Rights of the British America, in 1774, was clear and transparent as glass; "The God who gave us life, gave us liberty at the same time."

I Believe

that as I am in Trail for **Unequivocal False Claims** against me, I find strength from the Almighty God, who Created the Justice System of Truth from His Throne; and it's called Majestic Righteousness!

I Believe

that each Patriot and Loyalist and True American, will literally give their life for our country, called: United States of America. As for John Adams who wrote a letter of his commitment for Freedom and Liberty said: "Sink or swim, live or die, survive or perish, I am with my country from this day on. You may depend on it."

I Believe

that our Original Signers of our Sacred Transcripts made with pen and ink, gave their entire soul in public debates for America, and here is a small speech from the First Continental Congress Oct 14, 1774

"I am not a Virginian, but an American"

I Believe

that the Oceans that splash their waves upon the coastline beaches of America, repeatedly do this from sunrise to sundown; significantly reminding us, that God is Faithful to His Promises.

Deuteronomy 31:8

"For I will never leave you or forsake you"

I Believe

in the American Flag of our Nation and Country, for which many of men have died to have it raised upon their grave; and as a reminder of our American Heroes, this Motto on the first American Flag raised, by John Paul Jones on the flagship Alfred, December 3, 1775, said this on it…

"Don't tread on me!"

I Believe

as the clouds appear every morning, and at times there is a short thunder that darkens our skies, it is so amazing to see the sunlight burst forth and declare its true position; and as astonishing as it is, a Rainbow is made by water droplets, a true reminder that America is still a City on a Hill, by its Reflection of Perfection!

I Believe

that Abstinence is a Healthy Equation for Family Life, from Waiting to Taking. A true formula and description for anyone who waits for the opportunity of Marriage. For as an American Runner who disciplines himself and focuses on his goal to win, as he stays behind the line to start, and stays within his lane, just to obtain the Gold Medal of Marriage.

I Believe

in Truth and in Integrity, and Dignity as a Strong Mountain, for as the Sparrow who builds her nest high upon a tree branch, to protect her young; so then, this is how the Bridge of Excellence is made for America.

I Believe

to Live by Example and to Lead by Example, which provides a strong influence upon others, such as when Colonel George Washington appeared before **Congress in Uniform**. For when John Adams saw him, these are his words of him.

"O that I were a soldier! I will be. I am reading military books. Everybody must, and I will, and shall, be a soldier" letter to Abigail Adams

Nov. 29, 1775

I Believer

in True Confession, a Practice that is needed in America for Which It Stands, to bring us to our knees before our Heavenly Father; for Him to Embrace our Nation with His Righteousness and Holiness, that we would want and desire to be clean from our Sins… which means: "Missing the Mark!"

I Believe

Children should be Protected from Negative Strangers, as they are called, to be free to live a pure and chaste life; without interference by evil people, such as Pedophiles, who deserve severe punishment.

I Believe

American People have forgotten what it is and what it was, to Fight for Freedom from Tyranny, just as we fought against Hitler the Communist party; here is what John Peter Gabriel Muhlenberg said to his congregation in 1775, before leaving to join General Washington's troops in Virginia.

"In the language of the Holy Writ, there is a time for all things. There is a time to preach and a time to fight. And now is the time to fight."

TRUMP PROVERBS

CHAPTER 3

I Believe

in learning about Military Wars, in order that I may understand the Necessity To Protect our Nation America, for Which We Stand; War is a brutal force of death and life. Here is a quote from Thomas Pain in Sept 4, 1777 on The American Crisis.

"We fight not to enslave, but to set a country free, and to make room upon the earth for honest men to live in."

I Believe

that President George Washington was sent to Preserve Our Country, by Heavens Gates of Glory, for as he spoke of the desperate state of His Army just days before leading them across the frozen Delaware River, in a surprise attack on Hessian troops at the Battle of Trenton Dec 26, 1776. These words were written on a scrap of paper as he spoke to Benjamin Rush. "Victory or Death!"

I Believe

in great speeches based on Truth and Inerrancy, for Benjamin Franklin spoke at the Constitutional Convention Sept 1787 These are his words: "I have lived, Sir a long time, and the longer I live, the more convincing proofs I see of this truth—that God Governs the affairs of men. And if a sparrow cannot fall to the ground without His notice, is it probable that an empire can rise without His aid?"

I Believe

that America is unique and special and God has Blessed us with His Presence in everything we do, but also, He wants us to stay away from Un- American Values that can corrupt our Country United States of America; for President George Washington knew this very cleverly and clearly, and this is what he said:

Farewell Address Sept 17, 1796

"It is our true policy to steer clear of permanent alliances with any portion of the foreign world."

I Believe

Josiah Bartlett, a Founding Father, physician, statesman, a delegate to the Continental Congress for New Hampshire, and a "Signatory" to the Declaration of Independence, in Aug 1776. Doctor Bartlett Was a great man, and He was the first to affixed His Signature; and this is what is said of him, for He was a Man of Principle. "He had served his country faithfully in its hour of deepest peril, and the benedictions of a free people followed him to his domestic retreat."

I Believe

that each person in America can contribute, not money, but their Talent and Skill to make America Great, such as Francis Hopkins a New Jersey Congressman and a Signatory, who designed the American Flag. And also choose Betsy Ross a seamstress, to sew the flag, and including; she made uniforms and tents for the Continental Army, and here is a great picture of Personal Patriotism.

I Believe

that the Boston Tea Party story in 1773, indicates the passion of Americans to be free from Tyranny, to be Independent and Resourceful on its own. For here is a quote from John Adams Dec 1773

"The die is cast. The people have passed the
river and cut away the bridge"

I Believe

the man Josiah Quincy III was a wonderful American Patriot, who served in the Massachusetts Senate and in the U. S. House of Representatives and was a State Legislator, and finally Mayor of Boston from 1823 thru 1828. But what was very amazing and significant is that in 1993, a panel of 69 scholars ranked him among the ten best Mayors in American History. Now, are you able to do that on your own, for America and for your entire Family.

I Believe

true Leadership begins with how One Orders Directives and how One Instructs Directions and how One Provides Wisdom in the process of leading troops into battle; here is George Washington directing a letter to Colonel Burwell Bassett June 19, 1775

"I can answer for but three things: a firm belief in the justice of our cause, close attention in the prosecution of it, and the strictest integrity."

I Believe

our Government has the proper Checks and Balances, and all we need is to follow the Constitution of the United States and the Declaration of Independence; **for we the people** are the best Government under the Mighty Hand of God; here is a quote from Alexander Hamilton in April 30, 1781

"If the government is in the hands of a few, they will tyrannize the many: if in the hands of the many, they will tyrannize over the few."

I Believe

in life and in government, Honesty is the best policy for all humanity, and in being honest, is liken to a beautiful fruit tree, planted by a river of substantial flow; this means that the purity of water is the main essence to feed a tree to make it strong and healthy and to produce fruit for the hungry. Therefore, drink the cup of Integrity each and every morning.

Here is an interesting quote from Thomas Jefferson 1786

"The whole art of government consists in the art of being honest."

I Believe

that our Forefathers knew exactly how to run a New Government, for they were under the Tyranny from the British and were not represented properly, and we should be grateful that we have these heavenly transcripts, to teach us how to be Governed Properly. Thomas Jefferson said, July 4, 1776

"Governments are instituted among men, deriving their just powers from the consent of the governed."

I Believe

our Behavior In Public should be the same, as in our Home Life, this means that our Real selves and Ideal selves are partners in truth and in harmony with each other; so weather we are in Public view or in Homelife view, our Attitude and Character is as a Honey Bee, spreading sweetness where ever we go, as You Produce Sweet Honey.

I Believe

in Gods Wisdom, when He Created the grass blade, for it can withstand strong winds and not brake, for it can bend and sway and stay positively resilient; ... now, are you able to "Withstand" and stay strong with honor and integrity; and resist evil, Maintaining a Character of Utmost Honesty.

I Believe

in the Legacy of President George Washington, for He helped shape the Office of the Presidency and the Executive Branch, and was highly admired by all; **for he placed Honor at its Highest Identity and Lived it**, ... for the greater good of his Country, America.

I Believe

that God Almighty will give gifts and skills and talents to each and every person on earth, as for Thomas Jefferson, who signed Legislation to establish the United States Military Academy, May 16, 1802. And Major Sylvanus Thayer, who was considered the "Father of the Military Academy"

To Train Officers for War. He improved academic standards, instilled military discipline, and emphasized honorable conduct and officership; for the Nation's Defense and the wellbeing of the United States of America.

I Believe

each one of us, is Born for a Purpose and a Reason, and just look at history, such as Michelangelo who in 1508 began painting the Sistine Chapel the Vatican ceiling with the depiction of Adam and Creation. And Heinrich Von Dannecker in the 18th century in the height of his career, labored for six years to sculptor the Image of Jesus. So, in your life, or in the height of your career, what have you done for our History of America with your Purpose Driven Life.

Here is a quote by, Johann Wolfgang Goethe in Aug 23, 1787

"Without seeing the Sistine Chapel, one can form no appreciable idea of what one man is capable of achieving".

I Believe

every President of the United States, should have a personal walk with Jesus Christ, the Creator of the Universe, in that, the President should be able to Pray for our Nation with perfect humility and perfect publication; such as President George Washington, as he Prayed for our Country America.

"Almighty God: We make our earnest prayer that Thou wilt keep the United States in Thy holy protection; that thou wilt incline the hearts of the citizens to cultivate a spirit of subordination and obedience to government and entertain a brotherly affection and love for one another and for their fellow-citizens of the United States at large. And finally, that Thou wilt most graciously be pleased to dispose us all to do justice, to love mercy and to demean ourselves with that charity, humility and pacific temper of mind which were the characteristics of the Divine Author of our blessed religion without a humble imitation of whose example in these things we can never hope to be a happy nation. Grant our supplication, we beseech Thee, through Jesus Christ, our Lord. Amen."

I Believe

in Science as a great study and field of knowledge, for as Professor George Washington Carver, who discovered great resources from the Peanut to the Sweet potato and many other things; but he also attribute his discoveries from listening to God Almighty, and here is his Inspiration for us to know.

"The Lord always provides me with life changing ideas. Not that I am special. The Lord provides everyone with life changing ideas. These ideas are quite literally a treasure from the Almighty. It is up to each of us however, to choose and dig for the treasure."

—George Washington Carver

And what is so amazing and special about Science, is that God is the founder and main principle resource to all of nature and creation. May you become great and amazing as Professor George Washington Carver, for his life is a Perfect Example of Struggle as a Black Man and a Wonderful picture of a man who had Faith to **conquer all of his giants**. So go Conquer!

I Believe

in Bravery and Courage when all odds are against you, such as the **Tuskegee Airman**, The Tuskegee Airmen were the first Black military aviators in the U.S. Army Air Corps (AAC), a precursor of the U.S. Air Force. Trained at the Tuskegee Army Air Field in Alabama, they flew more than 15,000 individual sorties in Europe and North Africa during World War II. Their impressive performance earned them more than 150 Distinguished Flying Crosses, and helped encourage the eventual integration of the U.S. Armed Forces.

These men struggled and persevered and suffered for the Color of their Skin, but because these Men were created in the Image of the Almighty God, they were Victorious and Fruitful in their journey of Faith. Here is one sample of their Successes:

"that in more than 200 escort missions, the Tuskegee Airmen had never lost a bomber."

I Believe

in the Kitchen Table with our Families, where each Child is Enriched and Educated in Family Values as they eat and talk about almost everything, which is the Core Mountain of Character Building. Where everything begins and all things become; because, of the Dinner Table ready and set by Mom, this is where the Training to be Great in America begins.

I Believe

the Compass Teaches us many Lessons about Life and how we should live according to a Pure Value, in which when followed, survivors tell their stories of how they found a true and honest refuge in obeying what is genuine and accurate; though hand crafted by human hands, but yet worked with the forces of nature to save lives and many to return home from being lost at sea and land. **Here is a lesson**, if you ever feel lost, use the Creators Compass, and He will guide you directly home, where you belong.

I Believe

in the Growth of Trees, from the backyard to the countryside and into the deep forest, for they are a true inspiration and a milestone in world history, for they provide a chemistry of life, that enables mankind to embark on learning creativity and magnificence. For trees can grow through every season of life, from heavy snows to heavy rains and severe droughts of summer. And what is so amazing, is that tree branches always point straight up, to the clouds and the beautiful blue sky, which seems to tell us profoundly, that you will grow better if your attitude is focused on what is above where the Stars Shine Brightest, and discover the strength and encouragement of a growing tree, **as they Rest Under the Shadow of the Almighty.**

I Believe

in Education of the People, from early childhood and into adulthood, for knowledge is so valuable not to have, for it will Save your Life and encourage you to be well informed of information. We have Trained Doctors and Nurses and Aviation Pilots and Engineers and Scientist; and they all have one Common Denominator, to assist each other to improve one another and help one another.

James Madison, Founding Father and 4th President of the United States of America, said this of Knowledge.

"Knowledge will forever govern ignorance. And a people who mean to be their own governors must arm themselves with the power which knowledge gives."

I Believe

there was Incredible Wisdom that was given to Alexander Hamilton, for he was intellectually gifted and considered to be a great Scholar of Government. For he knew quite well, the secrets of Tyranny and Enslavement, for he was a Military Officer; but he also knew distinctly, what he was without the Wisdom from Above. Here are his last words, where he was fatally shot in a duel with Burr in July of 1804.

"I have a tender reliance on the mercy of the Almighty, through the merits of the Lord Jesus Christ. I am a sinner. I look to Him for mercy; pray for me."

TRUMP PROVERBS

CHAPTER 4

I Believe

people should Practice having an Honest Heart, before themselves and their families and their friends and in public opinion, and especially in front of the God who Created You. Just as restaurants provide good and great eating food to customers, they provide Excellent and Beautiful clean plates to eat off of; so in turn, in Congress and in Public Office, we should provide to our American people, a clean conscience and a clean plate before **.... we the people of the United States of America!**

Here is Benjamin Franklin, who was an American printer and publisher, author, inventor and scientist, and diplomat. One of the foremost of the Founding Fathers, and Franklin helped draft the Declaration of Independence, and was one of its signers. Represented the United States in France during the American Revolution, and was a delegate to the Constitutional Convention.

Here are his words:

> "Use no hurtful deceit; think innocently and justly,
> and, if you speak, speak accordingly"

"Think of three Things; whence you came, where you are going, and to whom you must account."

I Believe

homelessness is a problem in America, and should be resolved with Wise Counsel and Proactive Approach, where people are given an opportunity to work and help each other and provide for themselves. To Teach Them Self-Preservation and Dignity of Self, for it is very important for them, as they recover from their personal issues; **we stand by them to assist!** Here is a wise interlude by Benjamin Franklin, The Way to Wealth, July 7, 1757

"Laziness travels so slowly that poverty soon overtakes him."

"Dost thou love life? Then do not squander time, for that's the stuff life is made of."

—1746 Almanack

I Believe

sex Trafficking is a Sin in American soil, for this type of behavior and active action should not be happening in America. But this shows the Evil Nature of Human Mankind, and that is why We Have Laws to **Protect the Innocent;** so help me God and the rest of us in Congress, that we may seek Gods Wisdom and Grace and Mercy, that we are not Guilty of this severe crime and to put it in jail to **where it belongs**. God forgive us of this Sin that is happening in our Country, United States of America; we should cleanse this problem, before we are Judged Ourselves, ... for doing Nothing!!!!

Warning! You will give an account of your actions now, or after you die! Why? Because doing nothing about a serious problem like this, is … Unacceptable as Being in America and Being an American.

I Believe

in Teachers of our Nation, who Strive to be of Pure Excellence, for those who make it as a life career to be valuable as precious diamonds and precious stones of intelligence, that our Students, the kids of our Parents to inherit the Majestic Knowledge of Brilliance. To where our pupils will become Honor Roll Students and achieve great and wonderful things in life. **Such as Our Founding Fathers were Educated.**

Here is a Quote to Consider:

"Teachers write on the Hearts of their students, things the world can never erase."

I Believe

in the design of the American Engines that have amazing horsepower and can accelerate at high speeds, but what is very interesting, is that they need fresh air for them to operate, to get from one place to another; so, in your life, you need fresh air to get to one place you were **Born To Achieve**, such as your Goal in Life. But without the Breath of Life, you can accomplish nothing, so with that in mind, God your Creator is your Sustainer, and He knows the beginning from the end and the end from the beginning; He knows what you were Design For, and what you are Good At, so, step on the gas pedal, and make it happen, under the American Dream.

I Believe

in Superior Controls, as the transcripts of our Founding Fathers which were designed for our Nation. To Regulate and Set the Right Settings to Govern properly our country called America. Just as having a Thermostat in your own home to set the right temperature to live comfortably and happily; and for the true facts of life, we all need to Focus on what is True and Full of Dignity and of Wonderful Integrity. **This Wisdom is from our Founding Fathers**, who placed a Listening Ear to the Voice of their Creator, for He is the True Balancer of Life.

I Believe

in the convenience of Windows in our homes, to draw in the outside fresh air to push out the stagnant dead air. For when you do open the windows of your house, your life becomes happy and content, because of the outside fresh air, a Breeze of Joy. And because of that Freedom, We are given a Lesson on Elegance, for as the Beautiful Butterfly is able to dance and sing and land on every precious and breathtaking flower; we are able to also to Experience The Graceful Richness of Peace and Prosperity and the Blessings of Liberty, **by being involved with our own Loving Family.**

I Believe

in the History of our Nation, for which It Stands, for it holds all trues and all errors and reveals our true humanity, and oh yes, we have failed in many ways, but because of our Forefathers Vision and Dream to have a Theocracy in our Democracy, ruled by the majority; we the people have a incredible opportunity to maintain the Oaths of Office with a firm grip on diplomatic influence by Our Votes at the Ballet Box.

I Believe

in the Equal System of Justice, upon the Balance Of Scales where all facts and words and thoughts are evaluated with the Essence Of Purity, where people focusing with the Lens of Integrity, can see what is right and what is wrong. And for that reason, to identify what must be removed that is shameful and detrimental to our society, such as Communism and Abortion and Hatred against what is Good and Excellent in our Country called, America.

I Believe

in the Bible, the Word of God, which has been given down through the ages through history and through our Forefathers and unto us. A book put together in 1500 years from different authors and compiled into one source of divine wisdom; and which every book having a common theme of truth, and has been proven scientifically and historically and through archeology, and has never been disproven. So, the Burden of Proof is Upon You, who don't believe; and here is a Question for You:

"Can You disprove that God does not Exist, with facts and research of the entire universe!"

Unfortunately, you can't, and you will never be able to; … because God is Smarter than You!

Romans 1:20–22

"For since the creation of the world His invisible attributes are clearly, seen, being understood by the things that are made, even His eternal power and Godhead, so that they are without excuse.

Because, although they knew God, they did not glorify Him as God, nor were thankful, but became futile in their thoughts, and their foolish hearts were darkened.

Professing to be wise, they became fools.

I Believe

In the Declaration of Independence, ….

"We hold these truths to be self-evident, that all Men are created equal, that they are endowed by their Creator with certain unalienable Rights, that among these are Life, Liberty, and the pursuit of Happiness"

For this means, that We The People are to follow the Rules and Laws set up by the Governed to Protect the Free and Innocent from harm and danger; and here is where we have institutions of **Prisons to incarcerate those who brake the laws and who act out evil practices against the American People.**

I Believe

in every Season of Life, the Creator has a message and a lesson for each and every one of you, for as the Snow in the winter comes its way, and the Spring brings up beautiful and aromatic flowers to bloom, and the Summer to grow healthy vegetables and crops, and the Fall, to see all of the leaves on the trees turn bright orange and yellow; you wonder why so many changes and why so many wonderful things to see and experience, for it is because, His Wisdom is given to you, that you may learn His ways of the Beautiful Excellence of His Beauty, His Masterpiece of Brilliance.

Here are Gods Thoughts for You to Consider.

Isaiah 55:8–11

"For my thoughts are not your thoughts, neither are your ways my ways, saith the LORD. For as the heavens are higher than the earth, so are my ways higher than your ways, and my thoughts than your thoughts. For as the rain cometh down, and the snow from heaven, and returneth not thither, but watereth the earth, and maketh it bring forth and bud, that it may give seed to the sower, and bread to the eater. So shall my word be that goeth forth out of my mouth: it shall not return unto me void, but it shall accomplish that which I please, and it shall prosper in the thing whereto I sent it."

I Believe

that each person in America, **has a calling upon their life**, to do great things for your family and for your city and community. For as you step out in Faith and Hope, your children will see your Example of Trusting your God Given Purposes; that you will see your potential arise as the sunrise, for our Forefathers did the very same thing, They Trusted in the Almighty and Walked after His Leading, to Become Great Examples of Patriotism for America, the amazing Red, White and Blue.

I Believe

in the Attributes of Nature, for they testify of a Creator who is active in His Creation, for as the clouds form their beautiful mosaic with joy, and power and tremendous fervor, you will recognize the sound of the thunder and the evidence of that auditory, that lightening appears with a brightness of magnificent wonder. We as Americans, are we able to control or even contain this dynamic appearance, for all we can do, is understand, that His Love for us, is as what we see, His Magnificent Majesty of Excellence!

Job 37:2–5

"Hear attentively the noise of his voice, and the sound that goeth out of his mouth. He directeth it under the whole heaven, and his lightning unto the ends of the earth. After it a voice roareth: he thundereth with the voice of his excellency: and he will not stay them when his voice is heard. God thundereth marvelously with his voice; great things doeth he, which we cannot comprehend."

I Believe

government is the extension of our human desire, for our 'Chosen' People in Office, to declare in what we believe to be Proper and True. For we the people have place them into that Seat of Justice; **... may we humble ourselves**, to Seek and Ask that God Almighty to pick in our behalf, for the Future of our American Dreams, the Right Candidate!

I Believe

bitterness and hatred is an evil element, which destroys our democracy in the United States of America. For we Stand as a Nation of Law and Order and a Love for our Country, full of Honorable Dignity and overflowing righteousness; so, to survive our Founding Fathers Wisdom of the Ages, we must 'Hate what our Fore Fathers Hated', and that would be:

Communism and Tyranny and Abortion, and Sex Trafficking and Child Abuse and Perversion and Rioting and Bomb Threats and Confusing Children of their Identity and Abduction and Murder and Stealing and Lying and Prostitution and Pornography and Pedophilia and Treason; add as you wish!

I Believe

children should be Free of Negative Influence, information that would remove their innocence and beauty, they should be given the Right and Privilege, to learn and gather wisdom to live by, as our Forefathers did. For they were extremely intelligent and wise people, they strived and worked hard and gave up their lives to secure a magnificent way of life; **may we train our children, To Be Just Like Them**; "Historical Leaders of Justice!"

I Believe

in the Accuracy of the Bible, for Jesus Christ also a historical figure, gave us lessons to live by and thoughts to consider of his character, for in the book of John 13:1–5, it states two amazing things;

"He love them unto the end" and "began to wash the disciples' feet"; which is a gift from Him to us today in the United States of America, **and this is how we should live.** To love each other to the end, where nothing is left out in our relationships, and to be an Example to each other in Service to our Country; for once we practice these very simple truths, our lives and our society and our land will experience Gods Blessings and Favor upon us all.

I Believe

that when people talk to each other, **we are in the Presence of the Almighty at all times.** Yes, we are, and as we discuss our issues or our problems or trying to negotiate treaties between each other and our allies and enemies; **our words are the key to healing and harmony**, everything we say has a message and a meaning, which penetrates the heart of man when we talk.

Our Diplomacy are sentences of true merit and should be thought through for the safety of others, for I suggest, that if Honey is sweet from nature, and never changes its tune and style, then so should we. Here is a Bible verse to consider noteworthy.

Proverbs 25:11

"A word fitly spoken is like apples of gold in pictures of silver"

I Believe

in great and fantastic ideas, that can benefit our families and country into our future of America, for one, ... Cancer, which plagues our families and littles ones, especially our children. If you were to interview these fresh and vibrant kids and youth, and ask them about life, with Cancer, they would tell you **how valuable life is**; and the key question for them would be this, "Is Abortion necessary?" What do you think they would say? I suggest every woman who considers this decision, should be responsible as a Mother and be a Fantastic one.

I Believe

that each Lady in America, should be a Virtuous Woman of Great Character, one known to be trusted with truth, to be honorable in her conversations, to be greatly admired by all, to have a majestic attitude with her thoughts, to be noteworthy as a public servant to all, displaying dignity and justice in all of her actions. And her Main Goal in Life, is to provide comfort to every person she meets; and that she would become, the most Beautiful Red Rose in the World, having her Heart to have the Treasure of Excellence and a Fragrance never forgotten, as she walks in the Essence of Magnificence.

I Believe

in Justice, where equal fairness is given to each party, as a balance scale of weights are placed on either side, they are same in information and discussion, and should be and must be heard. How did Jesus place the Scales of Justice, when he was asked a very simple question:

Matthew 22:17

"Tell us therefore, What thinkest thou? Is it lawful to give tribute unto Caesar, or not?"

And Jesus answer was:

Matthew 22:21

"Render therefore unto Caesar the things which are Caesar's; and unto God the things that are God's."

Now question to You, my American Patriot?

Are You Paying Tribute to America and Giving the Things that belong to America: ... such as, Your Passion to Make America Great and Outstanding, using your God Given Skills and Talents and Honest Character? To where America is forever a City "Shining" on a Hill!

I Believe

no one who is American, should ever and never 'Compromise' when it comes to Honesty and Faith of the United States of America, for which it Stands.

Our Founding Fathers who gave their life and blood for our country gave us a True Example of Bravery and Courage to 'Stand Against' the tides of evil; that is why they came together as one Unity of Spirit and Force, to Win and Conquer with Victory … Tyranny of all sorts! John Adams, letter to Thomas Jefferson, August 24, 1815

> "As to the history of the revolution, my ideas may be peculiar, perhaps singular. What do we mean by the revolution? The war? That was no part of the revolution; it was only an effect and consequence of it. The revolution was in the minds of the people, and this was affected from 1760–1775, in the course of fifteen years, before a drop of blood was shed at Lexington."

I Believe

in America! The Beautiful, the Wonderful, the Majestic, the Magnificent, the Tremendous, the Fabulous, the Courageous, the Amazing Grace of Heaven; may we all humbly bow down before our Maker, who has placed America as the Beacon of Hope and the Lighthouse of Refuge to the World, and for the World.

I Believe

in the classic word called 'Integrity', where every ancient sculptor and artist always aimed at creating Jesus as its main passion to manifest Him clearly. Their craftsmanship has been displayed and is here till this day; their 'Integrity' is unto us as a Prism of Truth, just as a Rainbow never changes and it presents itself with pure 'Integrity', with colors that blend with natures beautiful flowers of the land. The reason for this artistic workmanship of majestic magnificence, is because, **Gods Handiwork does not compromise in His Excellency in any shape or form.**

TRUMP PROVERBS

CHAPTER 5

I Believe

in Genuine Wisdom, the same substance that our Founding Fathers used, such as making a wax candle by hand, until it was genuine to use as a candle to create light during the Evening Sessions Of Congress. Wisdom in its true essence, is divinely orchestrated with the excellence of honesty and dignity, for if each American which lives on the soil of prosperity and freedom, were to drink from this well spring of fragrance, the true results would make us all to think and live in this manner of existence as Our Founding Fathers.

James 1:17–18

"But the wisdom that is from above is first pure, then peaceable, gentle, willing to yield, full of mercy and good fruits, without partiality and without hypocrisy. Now the fruit of righteousness is sown in peace by those who make peace."

Galatians 5:22–23

"But the fruit of the Spirit is love, joy, peace, longsuffering, gentleness, goodness, faith, meekness, temperance; against such there is no law."

I Believe

that Our Freedom was the most expensive endeavor our Forefathers had taken upon themselves, for it cost each of them all of their Faith and Hope and Perseverance, and trust into the American people; who yet was able to see the future of True Liberty. We must never walk away from our Foundation of Excellence**, ….**

"In God We Trust"

George Washington First Inaugural Address April 30, 1789.

"The preservation of the sacred fire of liberty and the destiny of the republican model of government are justly considered, perhaps, as deeply, as finally staked on the experiment entrusted to the hands of the American people."

I Believe

in Hope of America and the Future of its Liberties and its remarkable prosperities, but though we all seek the Freedoms of our hearts and deepest desire to live with providence and peace, **we must all step forward, duty bound to secure our freedoms with the excellence of holiness**; we all desire to be Blessed and Benefitted with goodness, but since we are human mortals, we must all cleanse our hearts from evil and that which destroys and destructs our character, then we will be the People of God and rightly so.

George Washington, Farewell Address, Sept. 17, 1796

"The very idea of the power and the right of the People to establish Government presupposes the duty of every Individual to obey the established Government."

I Believe

in the Freedom of the Press, for without it, we are doomed for failure, for we are a people of thoughts and ideas and incredible intelligence, where with we have been endowed by our Maker with gifts and talents which we cannot deny; our inner wisdom of curiosity shows that we were designed to explore new ways and methods that grant us favor with humanity, and that is why sharing our stories and wonderful information, only enlightens us to be a Great and Mighty Nation.

Alexander Hamilton, Propositions on the Law of Libel. 1804

"The liberty of the press consist in the right to publish with impunity truth with good motives, for justifiable ends. To disallow it is fatal."

I Believe

our Forefathers were Gifted Men who experience tyranny and suppression to the point, that they cried out to the Living God of Liberty, and they were answered through Prayer, and as they contemplated the possibilities of this new found liberty, **the Spirit of God** began to give them wisdom

and discretion in how to format this new freedom with liberty. Thomas
Jefferson, letter to James Madison 1787

"I have a right to nothing which another has a right to take away. And
Congress will have a right to take away trial by jury in all civil cases. Let
me add that a bill of rights is what the people are entitled to against every
government on earth, general or particular, and what no just government
should refuse or rest on inference."

I Believe

in the Religious Right To Believe, and with that chosen belief, the way of
truth is known, as what is right to live by and what is wrong to neglect.
We the People have studied history, and has seen when a People begin to
Pervert Justice, and live as though the laws do not exist; well a Higher Law
does exist, and we are accountable to Him who established our country.
For we will all reap what we sow in life, **for it is an inevitable law of life**.

John Adams, letter to Francis van der Kemp Oct. 2, 1818

"I will not condescend to employ the word Tolerance. I assert that
unlimited freedom of religion, consistent with morals and property, is
essential to the progress of society and the amelioration of the condition
of mankind."

I Believe

Gods Word provides **answers and solutions and great common sense**,
when we needed most, and when it comes to our lives and what we have
done and accomplished, before our final day on earth; someone will give us
a tribute of our entire life, a final message of who we were, and an ending
of our legacy.

Psalms 119:33

"Teach me, O LORD, the way of Your statutes,
and I shall keep it to the end."

Henry Lee III, from his eulogy of George Washington, December 1799

"To the memory of the Man, first in war, first in peace, and first in the
hearts of his countrymen."

I Believe

the Sequioa Trees are the most beautiful Monarchs of its kind, and has lived
long enough to tell us what courage and bravery is all about, and to reveal to
us the purity of life and its necessity to growing old and mature and lasting
a very long time on earth; they have seen generations in their prime and
generations who failed, and they know what makes a prosperous society
and they specifically understand what healthy living is all about, especially
protecting our Nation from Arms Way.

Thomas Jefferson, letter to Colonel William S.

Smith, November 13, 1787

"The tree of liberty must be refreshed from time to time with the blood
of patriots and tyrants. It is its natural manure."

President Dwight Eisenhower

"America's problems might be easier to solve; if every American would
dwell more upon the simple virtues: integrity, courage, self-confidence,
and an unshakeable belief in his Bible."

I Believe

we must Never Lose Sight of Our Mission on earth as Americans, for we were born to live and destine to die, but with Dignity and Respect and into the grave. We have been given the privilege and the duty to live rightfully and carefully, before our last day on earth. If we choose to live out our lives in Injustice and Unfairness, then our Children has suffered and will continue. Unless, they take the Baton of Truth and Safe Justice and Support the American Way.

Thomas Paine, The American Crisis, No 4. September 12, 1777

"Those who expect to reap the blessings of

freedom must, like men, undergo the fatigue of supporting it."

I Believe

in Human Rights, as each and every one of us do, such as Unlawful Imprisonment, Torture, and Execution!

Declaration of IndependenceJuly 4, 1776 "We hold these truths to be self-evident, that all Men are created equal, that they are endowed by their Creator with certain unalienable Rights, that among these are Life, Liberty, and the Pursuit of Happiness……"

And here is the Answer for the Unborn Child, for nowhere in this Transcript of Truth, does it state the word, "Fetus"; it says the Creator Created

You, and that means from conception—Period! And Science, only explains the process—Period!

I Believe

in the Constitution of the United States and in the Declaration of Independence, written for the future of America. As our Forefathers attributed their Faith in God Almighty for our country, to protect it and secure it with Safety Measures against all Tyranny; Rules to Live by, which means that any people who chose to live unruly and against our Laws, are placed in Prison.

Here is a scripture text from the Bible on this subject. Romans 13:1–2

"Let every soul be subject to the governing authorities. For there is no authority except from God, and the authorities that exist are appointed by God. Therefore, whoever resists the authority resists the ordinance of God, and those who resist will bring judgement on themselves."

I Believe

those who Practice Homosexuality, Need Our Most Precious Help in America, though we may disagree in what lifestyle they choose, but still, they are Citizens of the United States of America. I find it rather disheartening, that they choose to continue in this Lifestyle, which they are not able to produce children by natural cohabitation, such as between Male and Female. But we must as Americans, come alongside them to assist them to **Choose Life, instead of Suicide**; may we all come to God Almighty and Pray for their souls to be at Peace with their Maker, and find rest and contentment in their lives, as long as they may live.

My Opinion only at this Point of Thought, due to the fact of so many partners, and each one is seeking True Love and Happiness; and due to their high sexual activity, their emotions become broken and hurt, and loneliness steps in, then depression, then, they feel unwanted. **Then it happens, they don't want to live anymore.**

More than 60% of suicide attempts among LGBQ people ...

Williams Institute
https://williamsinstitute.law.ucla.edu › Press

Jul 1, 2021—Bisexual respondents were about 1.5 times more likely to report **suicidal** thoughts and attempts, compared to **gay** and lesbian respondents.

I Believe

every person living in the Unites States of America **Contributes,** to the Growth And Building Up of America, for without their help, our country will **fall to ruins and crumble under the Hands of Not Caring.** For there was a Countrymen named, Robert R. Livingston who supported strongly the Declaration of Independence, but his name was not placed as a Signee, though he was an incredible Patriot; but yet, because of his good and great character, he was called upon to be a Chancellor of New York.

And had the Honor to administer the Oath of Office to our great Leader, President George Washington on April, 1789.

Where President George Washington before high heaven **gave his solemn pledge** to support the Constitution of the United States of America.

I Believe

in the Laws of the Land, for our Forefathers understood the complexity of tyranny and the effects of having no proper jurisdiction of control among the innocent people of America. For the Law is designed to Control Evil from spreading in a good and healthy society. We the People living in this marvelous country, is able to have Freedom to live happily ever after; therefore, we must embrace our Constitutional privileges and preserve our dedicated promises to live beautifully, **as we all take responsibility** to Vote for the Right Person for the Right Job, at the right time.

I Believe

what God says about me as His son in this world, and because of that, it gives me great confidence within myself to be magnificent like Him, as my Maker and Wonderful Example for living my life.

And to think how often does He think of me, **and you**, it says by King David, that as the number of grains of sand from the entire world, if we were to count them one by one, that is how many times He thinks of You and Me.

Psalms 139:17–18

"How precious also are they thoughts unto me, O God! How great is the sum of them! If I should count them, they are more in number than the sand: when I awake, I am still with thee.?

I Believe

in **the Providence of God Almighty,** for by His Spirit of Truth, He inspired our Forefathers to come together in Prayer and ask for Gods Leading Wisdom in forming the Constitution of the United States of America. Here are three great historical builders and architects and believers of our passed history that championed with victory—**America the greatest Nation in the World!**

George Washington Our First President

"The adoption of the Constitution, will demonstrate as visibly the finger of Providence as any possible event in the course of human affairs can ever designate it."

Daniel Webster Author 1st American Dictionary

"I regard it the Constitution as the work of the purest patriots and wisest statemen that ever existed, aided by the smiles of a benignant gracious Providence… it almost appears a Divine interposition in our behalf…"

Benjamin Franklin Founding Father of America

"I here so much faith in the general government of the world by Providence that I can hardly conceive a transaction of such momentous importance, as the framing of the Constitution… should be suffered to pass with out being in some degree influenced, guided, and governed by that…beneficent Ruler in whom all inferior spirits live and move and have their being."

I Believe

our **American English Language** was chosen and selected by God Almighty, and He chose a man called Noah Webster to produce it. Interesting to know, that he was a failed farmer, and an uninspired teacher. But as we know in life, God gave him heavens leading and guiding, for he became a state representative, a co-founder of Amherst College, a copyright advocate and a friend of George Washington. A Federalist and revolutionary who deeply loved our Country. For in 1828 he was credited for capturing the articulation of the English Language, and he persevered with hard work and dedicated service for America, that he championed from his heart with amazing passion; **and the American Dictionary was born.**

I Believe

God has chosen the Black Families of America to be the Saviors of the World; for they have been mistreated and purposely stepped on, inside the boundaries of America, but the Living God has brought us the Victory! In History, there was a group of Black Men who against all odds and all abuse and all neglect, persevered with courage from Heavens Door, they were called the:

"The Tuskegee Airmen" Facts Below:

"Our mission of escort was really the prime mission to carry out successfully and this we did. The 332nd became known as the best escort operator in the 15th Air Force. We never lost a bomber to enemy action of airplanes."—Gen. Benjamin O. Davis, Jr., Commanding Officer, 332 nd Fighter Group.

Also, a man named "Simon of Cyrene coming out of the country, and on him they laid the cross, that he might bear it after Jesus." Luke 23:26

Here we see, a Black Man carry the Cross of Jesus Christ!

Today! How we America needs, our Black

Brothers and Sisters, to carry us again into Victory, and escort us into the Promise Land of Peace and Safety; and to bring Justice and Righteousness back into American soil, … **and to Set us Free!**

I Believe

as Benjamin Franklin spoke this incredible statement, "The longer I live, the more convincing proofs I see that God governs in the affairs of men" and also stated:

Where he proposed in June 28, 1787

"that the Convention should be opened each day with Prayer"

Here we see how Prayer to God Almighty came to answer the Voices of Slavery and under Tyranny, when a Seamstress coming from work and entered a Bus in Montgomery, Alabama and 'Sat Down', because this 42-year-old woman was tired. Then a white man approached her and told her she was supposed to give up her seat for him, and she to get up and go to the back of the bus! She Refused!

This wonderful Lady was Rosa Parks, and which she ignited the Civil Rights Movement; She was Standing for her God Given Rights and did not back down. So, Standing for what is Right, and Praying to make it happen… how marvelous God is. **So, Stand, and make it Happen Again!**

I Believe

America is a place Inspired by Heavens front door, because all of the people in the whole world, send their children and relatives to live here and become educated and have a career, which in their 3rd world country, it is impossible.

We the People of America are a 'Chosen Group', as Paul the Apostle said in Ephesians 1:4

"According as he hath chosen us in him before the foundation of the world, that we should be holy and without blame before him in love."

I Believe

when I see the Heavens during the day and into the evening twilight, I discover, that our earth and our Milky Way Galaxy in the center of the massive universe of billions and billions of stars, shows we have an Architect in the family. As Mount Rushmore was designed by a Chief Architect named Gutzon Borglum, it was intended to celebration of not only these four presidents, **but also the nation's unprecedented greatness**.

It was a 14-year project, with 400 men, making each face a tall 60 feet; and in this great accomplishment, not one fatality occurred, which means, they did not lose not one soul. It is of great interest, that John Calvin a French theologian, Pastor and Reformer in 1536, repeatedly calls the Christian God, …

"The Architect of the Universe";

whom referring to Jesus Christ, and to also as Gutzon Borglum, … He did not lose any souls.

I Believe

our Military Soldiers who Stand for America and believe in its absolute democracy, and the United States Flag as its national symbol of which captures the power and glory of our nation; have sacrificed each of their lives with their entire body, mind, heart and soul. They all **March To War**, when our lives are threatened, and they do this with Loyalty, Dignity, Integrity, and pursue their enemy with justice and righteousness; for they have fully surrendered to their God Given Rights to Live, as a Gift to our Nation. May we never forget each of them, when they return to us at home, … in Spirit or in Body, and **Oh how we Love them all!** And God Bless each one of these Precious Ones who have served with a Gallant and Brave and Courageous Heart! **These Soldiers are truly our Knights in Shiny Armor.**

I Believe

in our Bill of Rights, it is a God Given Gift from heaven, for in December 15, 1791, it became law of the land.

For our Constitution begins with…

"WE THE PEOPLE, of the United States, in Order to form a more perfect Union, establish Justice, insure domestic Tranquility, provide for the common defense, promote the general Welfare, and secure the Blessings of Liberty to ourselves and our Posterity, do ordain and establish this Constitution for the United States of America."

Now the question You Must Ask Yourself? … 'could you on your very own wisdom and intelligence, create such a document as this?'

I Believe

that every person should have a good and great educational experience and graduate with honors, if they are able too. **The Pursue of Intelligence**, is a great honor and a beautiful opportunity to acquire while growing into adulthood. Knowledge is a very critical and important to have, for it gives you the fabulous pathway to create bridges where others have not been able to do; where others have failed in their quest, you have the perfect gift of wisdom, to develop and build a palace for others to abide in; **that the people of America is truly a Nation whom God is their Educator.**

I Believe

each America Person has been gifted to be great and prosperous with joy in their heart, for reason, America is a place where you can learn to be great and enthusiastic and filled with peaceful tranquility. For our Forefathers knew in advance, what it would take to be prosperous and have freely a divine providence of Blessings for each family in our Nation. This Treasure which is freely given, is Gods Hand upon your life!

Benjamin Franklin, Maxims and Morals 1807,

"Freedom is not a gift bestowed upon us by other men, but a right that belongs to us by the Laws of God and Nature."

George Washington, message to Quakers, 1789

"The liberty enjoyed by the People of these States of worshipping Almighty God, agreeably to their Consciences, is not only among the choicest of their Blessings, but also of their Rights."

Thomas Jefferson Declaration of Independence 1776 "All men are created equal"

Alexander Hamilton, speech at Constitutional Convention June 29, 1787

"There can be no truer principle than this—that every individual of the community at large has an equal right to the protection of government."

John Adams, letter to Abigal Adams, 1819

"Negro slavery is an evil colossal magnitude."

TRUMP PROVERBS

CHAPTER 6

I Believe

Our Forefathers had it right from the very beginning, but it took some time for others to understand Gods process of teaching mankind what Love is really like, for God not only created man and woman, but instilled within each of them His image and likeness as when Jesus spoke to His Father in Genesis 1:27

"Then God said, Let us make man in Our image, according to Our likeness…."

For in that statement, God Almighty would put His love in our Hearts for each other.

For in Matthew 22:36–39

"Teacher, which is the great commandment in the law? Jesus said to him, 'You shall love the LORD your God with all your heart, with all your soul, and with all your mind. This is the first and great commandment. And the second is like it; 'You shall love your neighbor as yourself."

If every person in America would have read and learned the Wisdom and Credibility of our

Forefathers, **then hatred and bitterness would not have existed at all;** Gods Love is the tremendous tidal wave for mankind, for he changes and moves within His people, and when He does, your life is changed Forever!

George Washington, letter to John F Mercer, September 9, 1786

"It being among my first wishes to see some plan adopted by which slavery in this country may be abolished by law"

So, if President George Washington, the Defender of Truth for Wishes and Dreams; … what are Yours for American to Stay Free from this kind of Abuse.

And since we are speaking for each American Soul, **have you considered the Child in the Womb?**

I Believe

in our History of our Nation, that God calls certain people to do His Bidding as the Creator of the Universe, for His reason. He extends His Hand to each of us through their lives, such as Pastor Billy Graham and Pastor Martin Luther King. Both were called at a time when our Nation needed God's

Forgiveness and Blessings. Quotes from each of them;

Pastor Billy Graham

"When wealth is lost, nothing is lost, when health is lost, something is lost, when Character is lost, all is lost."

Pastor Martin Luther King

"Darkness cannot drive out darkness, only light can do that, Hate cannot drive out hate, only love can do that."

Now as you read each of their best quotes during their lifetime, **they Both Had a Dream!**

"I have a dream that one day this nation will rise up and live out the true meaning of its creed—we hold these truths to be self-evident: that all men are created equal."

I Believe

that each of us in our lifetime, has to learn to survive for each other and for our fellowman, because if we do not pursue forward in behalf of America, our nation will fall and fail, so we must move forward and cross the Bridge Of Unity and Tranquility, where we each look eye to eye at each other and realize, how we need each other to survive, from our foreign enemies. Yes, we each have failures, and sometimes, it is our Character Building that needs perfection, then it happens; we learn to triumph and conquer our weakness and become a Historical Legend to our Families and Children. Two people in our History, changed and ignited loyalty and courage in a time when we needed it most, such as Winston Churchill and President Abraham Lincoln.

For one, it was Hitler who wanted to conquer and destroy everything that his ideology of communism wanted to consume; if he were to win, America would not exist as today with our Precious Freedoms.

Secondly, it was the evilness of our hearts, to keep people in slavery, because of the color of their skin—Black. But because of Truth in God, the Prayers

of the Black Families were heard: "The Emancipation Proclamation" …
was born.

Here is a Bible verse that Proves how Evil our
hearts are, when we Reject Gods Love for mankind and us.

Jeremiah 17:9

"The heart is deceitful above all things, and desperately wicked;
Who can know it?"

I Believe

that for those who believe that our Forefathers weren't or were Believers in
the God of the Universe, and having a Personal Relationship with Him,
must consider where your life is now, for if you died, where would you go?
For they all new that God was Just and Fair, and that is where they came up
with the Idea of the Constitution of the United States of America. They were
all driven by the scope and power of the Holy Spirit, and they all depended
on Gods Words as the final Absolute of all Answers.

Here is their Basis: 2 Timothy 3:16–17

"All Scripture is given by inspiration of God, and is profitable for
doctrine, for reproof, for correction, for instruction in righteousness,
that the man of God may be complete, thoroughly equipped for every
good work."

Here is Thomas Jefferson, regarding the issue of Slavery, Notes on the State
of Virginia, 1781

"God who gave us life, gave us liberty. And can the liberties of a nation be thought secure when we have removed their only firm basis, a conviction in the minds of the people that these, liberties are of the Gift of God? That they are not to be violated but with His wrath? Indeed, I tremble for my country when I reflect that God is just; that His justice cannot sleep forever."

I Believe

that the **Sex Trafficking issue in America is as Slavery,** and that Gods Judgement will soon become available, when those involved will die of a calamity or natural causes. We each will be held accountable for our lives, in what we do and what we have done.

In Romans 14:12 Paul said,

"So, then each of us shall give account of himself to God"

Jesus said: Matthew 12:36–37

"But I say to you that for every idle word men may speak, they will give account of it in the day of judgment. For by your words, you will be justified, and by your words you will be condemned."

Benjamin Franklin, An Address to the Public from the Pennsylvania Society for Promoting the Abolition of Slavery, and the Relief of Free Negroes Unlawfully Held in Bondage, 1782

"Slavery is such an atrocious debasement of human nature, that its very extirpation, if not performed with solicitous care, may sometimes open a source of serious evils."

George Mason, from debates of Constitutional Convention, August 22, 1787

"Every master of slaves is born a petty tyrant. They bring the judgement of heaven upon a country. As nations cannot be rewarded or punished in the next world, they must be in this. By an inevitable chain of causes and effects, Providence punishes national sins, by national calamities."

I Believe

Our Forefathers knew quiet well that the Almighty God of Heaven was calibrating their affairs as they were placing together the Constitution of the United States for America, for they began to see His Handiwork among them and His Perfective Beauty in their thoughts and actions with each other in their Sessions of Congress.

President George Washington, First Inaugural Address, April 30, 1789

"No people can be bound to acknowledge and Adore the Invisible Hand, which conducts the Affairs of men more than the People of the United States. Every step, by which thy have advanced to the character of an independent nation, seems to have been distinguished by some token of Providential agency"

Thomas Jefferson, letter to David Barrou, May 1, 1815

"We are not in a world ungoverned by the laws and power of a superior agent. Our efforts are in His Hand and directed by it; and He will give them their effect in His own time."

I Believe

all of our Forefathers read their Bible regularly and as often as they could, for they have stated numerous times what they think of Him, and what He is to them. Here are their own words about the God of the Universe!

Benjamin Franklin, Articles of Belief and Acts of Religion, November 20, 1728

"There is in all Men something like a natural Principle which inclines them Devotion or the Worship of some unseen Power."

George Washington, letter to William Gordon May 13, 1776

"No Man has a more perfect Reliance on the all wise, and powerful dispensations of the Supreme Being than I have nor thinks His aid more necessary."

Thomas Jefferson, letter to Benjamin Waterhouse, June 16, 1822

"Had the doctrines of Jesus been preached always as purely as they came from His lips, the whole civilized world would now have been Christian."

Thomas Paine, The Age of Reason, 1794–1795

"I believe in one God and no more, and I hope for happiness beyond this life. I believe in the equality of man; and I believe that religious duties consist in doing justice, loving mercy, and endeavoring to make our fellow creatures happy."

Thomas Jefferson letter to Henry Fry, June 17, 1804

"I consider the doctrines of Jesus as delivered by Himself to contain the outlines of the sublimest system of morality that has ever been taught, but I hold in the most profound detestation and execration the corruptions of it which have been invented."

I Believe

President John Adams was a remarkable and talented individual in history, for he served as Vice President for President George Washington and then became the second President of the United States of America in 1796. He also was the primary author of the Massachusetts Constitution in 1780, which influenced the United States Constitution, as did his essay Thoughts on Government. His insights are very incredible to behold, and these are his thoughts on two subjects.

One: "Our Constitution was made only for a moral and religious people It is wholly inadequate to the government of any other."

Two: "Have you ever found in history, one single example of a nation, thoroughly corrupted, that was afterwards restored to virtue? And without virtue there can be no political liberty.

I Believe

the wind speaks for itself, for it can be destructive and meaningless, for in its inner character, it has the power to do as it wills, and its identity is found in the Hand of His Maker and Creator. And it has the magnitude to demonstrate a wonderful gentle breeze, to where even a child is comforted with its presence and existence; but when it presents itself and stands in front of the Prince of Peace, it hears a gentle voice and a soothing romance, as an invitation to come home, "Peace be Still" So, if the Wind can hear His Voice and Follow His Leadership and be reduced to Peace; then why do we have so many Gangs, that just don't Care at all? Is it possible, that the Father in the Home, has Failed His Responsibilities, and did not give his Children the Peace that comes from Heaven.

I Believe

in the Power of the American Flag, for it is a symbol of our American Heritage, of who we are as a People! For every war that has been ignited, it has been based on bitter hatred for America, a land of the Free, a home of Patriots who stand for justice and righteousness and Love for our Country. Knowing that each Star represents each of us, and the colors of our beautiful flag; White signifies purity and innocence (our Families and Children) Red represents hardiness and valor (our Military Forces to Protect) Blue stands for vigilance, perseverance, and Justise (to believe and trust in our laws of the land).

In 1954, in response to the Communist threat of the times, President Eisenhower encouraged Congress to add the words "under God' creating the 31 word pledge we say today.

"I pledge allegiance to the Flag of the United States of America, and to the republic for which it stands, one Nation under God, indivisible, with liberty and justice for all."

I Believe

in the Faith of little Children, who will against all odds can survive, even a holocaust, and to imagine its emotional tension of scares and abuse and inflicted pain upon them. They should not go through these things, for they should be protected under the Shadow of the Almighty with Prayers and Promises; so here is a Precious little lady named: Rudy Bridges who was 6 years old and went to school in an all-White Elementary School in the South. She was Black, and very Beautiful indeed, and she made and changed history, by simply following her Teaches lessons and learning to be a True American defending the Constitution of the United States of America, For Which We All Stand! And because of Her Experiences, She established, "The Ruby Bridges Foundation" to promote "the values of tolerance, respect, and appreciation of all differences."

I Believe

in the Words of Jesus Christ, who died for our sins and rose from the dead, and who sits on His throne waiting for us to come home, for He is the Author and Finisher of our Faith and the Kingsman Redeemer of our souls; for when He said, …

John 14:6

"I am the way, the truth and the life, No one comes to the Father except through Me."

He described our True American Heritage, and that is why America exist today; ….

"In God We Trust".

He made the 'Way' for America to be born and brought forth, He made 'Truth' to be the bases of our American judicial system, He made 'Life' that we may live in harmony with Him and be at peace with His wonderful teachings, and with each other.

I Believe

in the Almighty, for His Creative Genius in how He Created the World and all of its imaginative expressions and impressions of His divine Wisdom. When He placed the stars in the sky, He gave each of them a unique name, when He placed the electromagnetic field, an imaginary line points due North or South using a Compass, when He created insects, he gave us His inside Wisdom to learn Objective Lessons of Life and how to apply them to ourselves; such as the Butterfly, who are place inside a Cocoon, to learn to 'Struggle' in order to survive life. This imagery is so spectacular, that a Butterfly must learn to exercise its instinct to 'stretch and push' and force itself out of the Cocoon, and once it does, it waits for the sunlight to give it warmth and strength and faith, to fly into the air with such beauty and majesty and harmonizing with nature.

I Believe

the Titanic would have been spared, if the communications directed to the Titanic, would have been received with courtesy and justly so.

This tragedy was massive, it killed over 1500 people in a matter of hours, and many stories are spoken of heroism and selflessness and sacrifice, but what is very significant to my heart, is that God was sought after during this episode of sadness.

For there was a Band of Musicians Violinist, and they played to calm their nerves and stresses being near the point of death. They played: "Nearer, my God, To Thee" and people sang as they sank into darkness. I believe strongly in my heart, that we as Americans serve a great and amazing God, who taught us to love one another in crises and in sorrow; and to sacrifice for the cause of the better good.

John 15:13

> "Greater love hath no man than this, that a man
> lay down his life for his friends."

I Believe

children should be Trained and brought up with proper Virtues and Moral Values, for if we don't, we will raise a group of unruly and defiant and rebellious people, who will eventually destroy themselves, over greed and arrogance and pride.

Our schools in America, also, are partially responsible to guide and direct our children when they are in school and not at home, so with that mentioned; We the people of the United States of America, are duty bound to bring up a Nation of Legendary people, who will create for us a better America to live in, with peace and tranquility and a greater love for each other.

Proverbs 22:6

> "Train up a child in the way he should go, and when he is old he will not
> depart from it"

Ephesians 6:1–4

> "Children obey your parents in the Lord, for this is right. Honor your father and mother, which is the first commandment with promise. That it may be well with you and you may live long on the earth. And you, fathers do not provoke your children to wrath, but bring them up in the training and admonition of the Lord."

I Believe

war between nations is horrible and tragic, for it destroys the hearts of mankind, but because of bitterness and hatred between countries, we all suffer ruin and hope. America wants Peace with all Nations, and since we are a God-Fearing Democracy at heart, the God we serve is our Supreme Protector and Friend. Therefore, as our Forefathers also sought for peace, they still had enemies who did not serve the God that we serve till this day.

Benjamin Franklin, letter to Josiah Quincy III, September 11, 1785

"I rejoiced at the return of peace. We are now friends with England and with all mankind. I hope it will be lasting, and that mankind will at length, as they call themselves reasonable creatures, have reason and sense enough to settle their differences without cutting throats. May we never see another war! For in my opinion there never was a good war or a bad peace."

Benjamin Franklin letter to John Adams, October 12, 1781

"I have never known a peace made, even the most advantageous, that was not censured as inadequate, and the makers condemned as injudicious or corrupt. "Blessed are the peacemakers" is, I suppose, to be understood in the other world, for in this they are frequently cursed."

I Believe

in the Book of Proverbs, Solomon the author was one of the greatest men on earth, who understood many things at large, but at the end of his life, he did not heed his own warnings for living proficiently and lost his passion. Wisdom in itself, is living with a skill of prudence and discretion, to where

all of your decisions in life; are remarkably done with wise counsel, as the
wings of integrity

painting dignity upon the canvas of advice; and everybody benefits from
you to them. And I find that asking God Almighty for His Wisdom is even
better. So, to be the Greatest Person on earth and do well, I suggest you seek
and ask the God of the Universe for His personal agenda on decision making.

James 1:5

"If any of you lack wisdom, let him ask of God, that giveth to all men,
liberally, and upbraideth not; and it shall be given him"

Proverbs 9:9–10

"Give instruction to a wise man, and he will be yet wiser; teach a just
man, and he will increased in learning. The fear of the LORD is the
beginning of wisdom; and the knowledge of the holy is understanding."

I Believe

each of us in our lives, Mimic Someone we have seen that impressed us to
make us better or improve our attitude and character. For we have relatives
and family members who in their lives did something so heroic, that it
impacted us mentally and emotionally, in fact, including spiritually; our
Fathers and Mothers who sacrifice for us, when we were in rebellion in our
teen years, including our Gracious Grand Parents who continually were
by our side. May we ever be like the best of them and live out our lives as
Instruments of Integrity for the benefit of mankind. Here are two Bible
verses that may help you.

Ephesians 5:1–2

"Therefore be imitators of God, as beloved children, and walk in love, just as Christ also loved you and gave himself up for us, an offering and a sacrifice to God as a fragrant aroma."

Philippians 3:12

"Brethren, be followers together of me, and mark them which walk so as ye have us for an example."

I Believe

our Farmers are genuine Patriots of America, for they are the most sufficient and efficient and proactive group of people known to mankind. For without their skills and natural abilities to understand the Farming Trade, **America would starve to death**. They are the True Stewardship of our Country, for they are not only dedicated to their workmanship, it is a life long purpose for them; they understand their own personal calling upon their life, to Feed the Nations as such and provide for the hungry and destitute. We should be Thankful and Blessed that our strategic Farmers are not only dedicated to its customers, but is loyal to the United States of America, … Oh how we should Pray for them and thank them. Amen!

I Believe

our Medical Community of Doctors and Nurses and Physicians and Surgeons and all that is involved with saving lives, are a Heavenly Anointed Group of People in Our Nation. With all of the technology and sophisticated equipment that they use and need in their performance; just to save one life! For as the

Paramedics who are the First Responders to Rescue a life when called upon, they not only do a good and a great job, they **Exceed the Call of Duty**, to make sure that each life they meet in turmoil is Rescued; and their goal and main objective, is to make sure they return home and continue living their life, until their time is done.

I Believe

our Children are the Next Saving Generation for Americas Future, for without them and their learning of the American Values, we will have no American Nation. We as Parents must adhere to the Value of Loyalty and the Treasure of Sacred Honor being a Parent. You have been entrusted to care for your children, and to Teach them and to Guide them and Show them the Way of Godly Principles that Built this Nation. Our Forefathers paved the way of proper education and proper government control; for they gave unto us a Constitution and a Declaration of Independence to secure this Nation as an Elite Country, and one that is Blessed by the Almighty God of Heaven.

I Believe

in the Power of the Pen, as an Executive Privilege to sign into law, that which is good and wholesome and beneficial to mankind, to Build up America.

Abraham Lincoln did just that, for there was a man named, Gordon, who later became a Sergeant in the African American Regiment and fought in the Civil War. And during his medical examination, they discovered his scarred back of being whipped and beaten, by his slave owner. So, he allowed a photographer to take a picture, and the scene shocked the country, and it was used by the abolitionist to push to stop Slavery. So, Abaham Lincoln signed into law the 13th Amendment into our Constitution of the United States of America.

Peter (enslaved man) known also, as "Whipped Peter" or Poor Peter. Can be researched for more detail of this account.

I Believe

the reason America is such a Great Country, is because it is Blessed of God, for through Him the Father of Heaven influence our Founding Fathers with His Presence to be the greatest country in the whole world. God gave Divine Wisdom to each Signer of the Constitution and the Declaration of Independence; and because they responded in simple Faith in Him, He granted their request.

And from then on, we have good jobs with good money to pay our bills and save for vacations and buy a house. Here is a beautiful quote from the Bible:

Ecclesiastes 3:13

"And also that everyman should eat and drink, and enjoy the good of all his labor, it is the Gift of God."

I Believe

in sweet potatoes, for they are tasty and sweet and healthy all together, and for an interest of beautiful facts in our history; their was a very cleaver Black Man named, Dr. George Washington Carver, who through his personal research was able to develop 100 uses in culinary, industrial, and commercial products, including 300 uses from the peanut. But what most people don't know about his life, was that his father died before he was born and his Mother and Sister and himself were kidnapped by raiders, and he was the only one found, for a trade of a horse. He was raised by white parents, who taught him how to read and write and do chores and gardening. Still His History, was a strong struggle because of His color, and this is a must read. My question to you is this: 'are you able to succeed as he did, under his circumstances, and survive and become world famous and be a Great Gentleman of Faith and able to help his world before he died. Here is his epitaph:

"He could have added fortune to fame, but caring for neither, he found happiness and honor in being helpful to the world."

I Believe

music is a Gift From Heaven, for it has the power to carry you into another world of peace and tranquility, and to emotionally move you into what is true. When I think of the song, "Amazing Grace" and discover the words by John Newton, who was a Captain of a Slave Ship; and to consider the melody is referred to as, 'Unknown'.

Here is a Quote:

"On March 10, 1748, Newton was steering his ship through a fierce thunderstorm when he Prayed to God. When he made it through the storm, he attributed his safety to the Grace of God. It was this event that started his conversion and led to him eventually becoming an Anglican clergyman in 1764."

I believe the 'melody' came from the suffering Black Slaves being carried in the Slave Ship; as they were groaning and suffering; all they could do was hum their miseries away…. I Believe God was listening to our Black Men and Woman, and heard their plea. Amazing Grace!

TRUMP PROVERBS

CHAPTER 7

I Believe

our God who Created the entire Universe, has a very unique Resume on file; in fact, all the Angels are all jealous, because they can't make it as good as He can.

Well, His address is as follows:

Yahweh Jesus Christ The Great I AM
Billions Majestic Galaxy Ave.
Holiness, White Throne 88888

He was educated by being Home schooled, and later attended University of Holiness and graduated with Honors as Valedictorian. His Major is Excellent Love and Wisdom, and His PHD is in Perfect Virtue and Helping Others become Perfect, like Him.

His first assignment was Earth, and their He created Adam and Eve and gave them their first duties and only one directive and protocol; and they miserably failed and lost the Trust Deed of the earth; and it was foreclosed and bought by Satan, Lucifer, Son of the Morning Star. So, Jesus has come after us to rescue us from our temptations and failures and mistakes and wrong decisions. Currently, we have wars of hatred and social injustice, Marriages breaking up, aborting His children alive in the womb, and the love between us is becoming cold and callous; which also drugs and prostitution and sex trafficking is on the rise. Jesus Christ is knocking on the door of your heart, and He doesn't care, if you are messed up or have ruined your life. He doesn't care if you are Ray, Lesbian, Transgender, Upside/Down, Straight, Crocked, Lopsided, Deformed, Crippled, Deaf, Blind and or Ignorant. **He loves you and wants you to be His!** He loves you so much, He will step into your heart and completely 'Decorate your life from the inside'. Where there are walls of shame, He will put His pictures of Grace of Peace. If your soul has been beaten down with abuse, He will put His Joy inside your heart with flowers of amazing fragrance, where the Angels will gather around to enjoy. And finally, if you have been neglected and cast away in the streets; He will come along side you and help you along the way….Forever!

Here is Jesus Christ simple request for You!

Matthew 11:29–30

"Come unto Me, all you who labor and are heavy laden, and I will give you rest. Take My yoke upon you and learn from Me, for I am meek and lowly in heart, and you will find rest for your souls. For My yoke is easy and My burden is light."

I Believe

each of us in life, Learn From Each Other as we grow up and journey into humanity, then as life goes on, you begin to Make Choices for Yourself.

After your choices, you begin to examine your intellectual moves and you ponder and evaluate them; then you realize how great they are or how dumb they are. Right now as I write this illustration; you are where you are and you are what you are by your Choices you made yesterday or today. If you are not Happy or Content with your Choices, then you need to **Practice the Perfect Choice!** America was built by people who made good and bad choices, but, the ones who made the: "The Perfect Choice" became the successful ones and made it well for themselves and for their families. Our Nation is made up of Immigrants, who came here on a whim and decided to stay for Freedom of Religion and Freedom of Speech, and Freedom of Prosperity, to get a good job and become wealthy and free, and to Raise A Great Family. **By doing this, I believe is the 'The Perfect Choice."**

I Believe

our Attitude in America, should be like our Grand Mother, who always was watching out for us and making sure we were doing the right thing at the right time in our lives. She was a Watchful Eye for us and kept her focus upon each of us when you and I were visiting her. She was and is our **Icon of Life** and our personal Super-Hero and Power Ranger; for she represented what is Holy and Virtuous, and what is right and wrong and what is best for us. Grandma was like an Amazing Grace Saint in our household, she Prayed for us, interceded to God Almighty, the Dude who made the Stars for us to see at night, and the Main Man of Heaven. She made sure we were on the right track of life, for it not, she would definitely keep us informed, even if she had to grab us by our ears and hair and almost strangle us to push us into Great Character. In fact, her ultimate goal for you and I, was to make us into the Image of Jesus Christ, because she knew, what was best for us. So, question to you is; "What is best for your life, Grandma's Wisdom or yours."

I Believe

in the Almighty, because He made the Universe, and for the Stars at night prove His existence, but we think we know everything, because we have arms and legs and a brain; and no one can catch us? But unfortunately, we can only live for a short time on earth, or if we get a bad disease from our behavior and we die with aids or cancer, what then? We and I, should once in a while walk into a big country park or go into the woods or into the high forest, …. and reunite yourself with Him. As You know, **He is harmless**, and in fact, He is gracious and kind and a best friend when You Are In Need! I have been found of Him, or I have found Him, nonetheless, He has a better life for you, then you have for yourself; He sees the Beginning of your life and the End of your life, so if He does, then let Him take the **Helm of your Soul,** and the center of your total being to make you Famous for the Worlds Sake…. Your Heart!

I Believe

our lives have Merit and Value and a distinct destination before we give up our Soul! We each have an 'Index', yes, an 'Index' in and on each of us. We were born for a True Purpose, since our life is not fully understood where we belong, we need to see some proof, why we exist? Currently now, the number one selling book in the entire world, that continually exceeds every other book is,? Your Right! The Bible! With an estimated 5 Billion copies sold and distributed. So, with that said, with 37 Million churches in the world, and 2.5 billion Christian denominations globally. Now you have to ask yourself? Why so many Believers in God Almighty? Well, the answer is obvious, as our Forefathers came together by Gods Handiwork, they saw the future of America and the world, so they produced the Constitution and the Declaration of Independence referencing God as the Author and Finisher of their Faith. Now, do You Believe you have an 'index'… for it is the spectrum of your life?

I Believe

The words of our Forefathers are the Foundation of our Strength of America and which we owe them privilege. Here are two in reference to the Constitution when it was drafted:

John Adams, 2nd President of the United States.

"I first saw the Constitution of the United States in a foreign country...
I read it with great satisfaction, as the result of good heads prompted by good hearts, as an experiment better adapted to the genius, character, situation, and the relations of this nation and country than any which had ever been proposed...I have repeatedly laid myself under the most serious obligations to support the Constitution...What other form of government, indeed, can so well deserve our esteem and love!"

Dr. Samuel Adams, a Revolutionary Leader ... etc.

"The sum of all is, if we would most truly enjoy the
gift of Heaven, let us become a virtuous people:

then shall we both deserve and enjoy it. While, on the other hand, if we are universally vicious and debauched in our manners, though the form of our Constitutuion carries the face of the most exalted freedom, we shall in reality be the most adject slaves."

I Believe

the Lincoln Memorial is our History of who we are as a People, and what we Believe in as Americans.

It Honors Abraham Lincoln as the 16th President of the United States, and the virtues of tolerance, honesty, and constancy in the human spirt. And Lincolns statue as the Leader who "Saved the Union" was paramount. The Lincoln Memorial symbolic use of fasces the unifying feature of the memorial emphasizes the importance of the union of the states and Lincolns role in Preserving the Union. And lastly, He issued the Emancipation Proclamation that **declared forever free those** slaves within the Confederacy in 1863. Which also, in Lincolns Temple, we are a grateful nation who honors a Martyred President who guided the country through Civil war and freed 4 Million enslaved persons.

Now, can you accomplish the same agenda today as He did, but in our Public School System…?

I Believe

every American should always be in 'Ready Stance' to protect our American Rights as a Nation. We must always Fight and Resolve any conflict that affects and effects our Constitution of the People.

We must always be Standing Tall as a Christian Nation, for which our Forefathers Founded with the origination of our Bible in Hand. For every Forefather was not ashamed to be called: "A Believer"! If you are an American, what kind of Believer are You? Reason I ask, is that the Nations around us, are 'Communist and Anti-America', they want to destroy us for our Stance on God! Right now, China, Iran, Russia and other miserable enslave countries Hate America, **and that's all they Believe in; Hatred!** They are Called: "Hatred Believers", because they are Tyrants by nature. So, Choose today, what You decide to do, Stand for America or Fall for the Hatred of our Country.

I Believe

in the Essential Wisdom of our Founding Fathers, for they sought after a better way and method to Rule A Country with peace and safety. We are indebted to them and owe them our prestige and respect and honor, for they laid the groundwork of the United States of America, and for which We Stand! We have been handed a Gift from Heaven, Gods beautiful handiwork of grace, and which He the Master of the Heavens has graciously handed to us individually. He has given to each of us Rights to live by, Freedom Rights to embrace and encourage us to have by, and Freedom Laws to Protect us from arms way. May we humbly come together and celebrate our Victory of our Nation and the Preserver of our lives, living under the Shadow of His Wings, full of Grace and Truth for each and all of us, who are Americans.

I Believe

we must not forget, where American came from; just as the Jews when they were delivered from the German Nazi concentration and extermination Camps, called: The Holocaust, a place of genocide in the world! The location Auschwitz is where it all happened! What is so evil to discover and learn from this, is a person called: 'the Angel of Death'! …a Physician named Josef Mengele, who conducted inhumane and deadly medical experiments on prisoners at Auschwitz. He became the most notorious of the Nazi doctors who conducted experiments at the camp. Mengle was nicknamed the 'angle of death'. He is often remembered for His presence on the selection ramps at Auschwitz. He believed in Nazi Racial Theory! And because of this, they killed over 6 million Jews, by systematic murder, gas chambers, mass shootings, deliberate privation, disease and brutal treatment, and including weather deaths. But on record, a man named Mao Zedong killed 65 million Chinese for reason to create a "socialist" China. He killed 'Intellectuals' and he buried alive 46 thousand scholars and China was called: "House of Fear"! And he established a system of 1000 forced labor camps throughout China. So, with this information of other countries, who were Faithless in God, We the people of America, do Believe in God, who is our Refuge and Hope; … so let us never forget where we came from?

I Believe

in Public Justice and Fair Justice and Social Justice and including Transparency Justice; … all based on Truth and Honesty and Explained with Pure Integrity. Here is a statement made, in comparing United States of America to the Roman Empire, **before it fell!**

"A great civilization is not conquered from without until it has destroyed itself within. The essential causes of Rome's decline lay in her people, her morals, her class struggle, her failing trade, her bureaucratic despotism, her stifling taxes, her consuming wars."

If you compare the Fall of Rome to the United States of America, what do you see in America that have the same symptoms and weaknesses and failings and equivalence.

My suggestion is this, let the Facts Speak for Themselves, and including this:

"Are You the Cause of Our Country Failing?"

I Believe

that Anger and Bitterness and Hatred should not exist in America, the reason Christianity is the answer for this; Christ introduced His love for human mankind. He said:

1 John 3:16

"By this we know love, that he laid down his life for us, and we ought to lay down our lives for the brothers."

John 15:13

"Greater love hath no man than this, that a man lay down his life for his friends."

If we are to take the words, Brothers and Friends mentioned in Scripture, then this means, that each of us which are made in the Image and Likeness of God Almighty, then are we to Honor and Respect each other; … no matter what we are or what we have become in society!

But, each of us must take Full Responsibility in what becomes of America, after our Choices and Decisions we have made for our benefit and our best interest. Unfortunately, our decisions in life, will have a Positive or Negative impact upon our Society. May we Each Chose what is Perfect and Upright that would Build Up America, and make it last into the next millennium.

I Believe

the White House is a Symbol of Truth and Dignity and Stands for Righteousness and Justice. But if you consider the workings of Michelangelo in what he constructed as admiration and wonder and spender; what symbol did he present to the world? The Sistine Chapel, depicting the Book of Genesis. The Pieta, depicting Mary weeping over the dead body of Jesus. The Last Judgment, depicting the Second Coming of Christ and the Final and Eternal Judgement of God of all humanity. And what were his remarks on all of his Makings of Beauty.

"The true work of art is only a shadow of the
divine perfection" Michelangelo

I Believe

that Mother **Teresa**, an Albanian-Indian Catholic Nun and the Founder of
the Missionaries of Charity, was a fantastic and outstanding and wonderful
Lady. She revolutionized wherever she went, and it is known that she began
her Work of God, helping those most in need. For she is a worldwide icon,
for her work in India, and for helping others with her devotion of selfless
dedication and unwavering commitment to humanity and which we all
admire her Christlike Behavior and representing Jesus Christ as the Savior
of the World.

Her primary role, was to love and care for those persons nobody was prepared
to look after; such as the poor, sick, orphaned and dying. She went after
the lost, who could not help themselves, at the age of 18 years old. She was
called: "The Saint of the Gutters!" At the end of her 45 years she passed
into Heaven's gate with complete and pure satisfaction.

On earth she earned: 100 Awards for her work and 700 Prizes for her
charity; … she is the most awarded person in the XXth century. Now, are
You able to Match her Performance and Improve our Worlds condition,
for we need more people like her, and I think as an American, 'Others Like
You' should be lineup to bat, So Batter Up!

I Believe

in Scientific Research for the betterment of the American People. Currently
now, we don't have a medicine to cure Cancer. HIV which is a severe death
procedure, we don't have a cure for this disease, but including other STD's

gonorrhea, syphilis, hepatitis, we have treatments available to help and assist patients. We the People of America, must realize, that STD is a serious threat to our Society, and with the cross-over of gender experimentation among consenting adults, our **Nation is in Hugh Trouble**?

We Have The Right as Americans to do as we please, but remember, our Freedoms come with a Cost and a Price! Our Military men and women who have fought and died for our Country, to keep us Safe and Secure;

> "We are dying ourselves because we are playing with fire, the same fire that our Military has faced; Death!"

Please Hear My Plea? Keep yourself … 'Pure'…, by practicing Abstinence and Protecting Yourself with only One Partner; not hundreds, which often the problem mostly is.

I Believe

in the Parables of Jesus Christ, for He taught with Wisdom and Truth, for He said in:

John 14:6

> "I am the way, the truth, and the life. No one comes to the Father except through Me."

Jesus was very clear in His dealing with Truth for People, for they and we all need clear and honest instruction as to where to go in life. We learn as we go, and discover our Purpose in God's Plan for eternity. A Parable is designed to sculpture an illustration in our minds, a poetic picture of Truth, a rainbow after a desert storm, in order to explain it. Here is a classic illustration.

Matthew 7:24–27

"Therefore whoever hears these sayings of Mine, and does them, I will liken him to a wise man who built his house on the rock: And the rain descended, the floods came, and the winds blew and beat on that house; and it did not fall, for it was founded on the rock. But everyone who hears these sayings of Mine, and does not do them, will be like a foolish man who built his house on the sand; And the rain descended, the floods came, and the winds blew and beat on that house; and it fell. And great was its fall."

I Believe

in the Historical Brilliance of the Coastal Lighthouse! For from its inception, it gave Captains of ships and Sailors of cruse boats to navigate their way through the darkness of the great deep, the ocean. How we are thankful and appreciative for the engineers who studied and designed these great and magnificent Candles of Truth to save lives from destruction. For as you go along these wonderful and splendid Prism Castles; you fall in awe of their Majestic Excellence, for they stand alone and remain strong and courageous, and they do what they were designed to do; … **Shine in the Darkness**! It is of Spiritual Value to every American who believes in the Maker of Light, who is the Light of the World. And who invites you to be a Candle of Peace and Grace. For Jesus said:

Matthew 5:14–16

"You are the light of the world. A city that is set on a hill cannot be hidden. Nor do they light a lamp and put it under a basket, but on a lampstand, and it gives light to all who are in the house. Let your light so shine before men, that they may see your good works and glorify your Father in heaven.

I Believe

that Mentoring others as Life Coaches and as Wisdom Facilitators is a Brilliant way to Build Up Family, Friends and Country.

America was Built by Strong Advice Given to each other!

Yes, wise counsel and courageous insight of intelligence, that others would grasp the meaning of life. Every Father and Mother instructs their children with great manners of diplomacy, including being honest and trustworthy and working hard as a strong ethic. The Family believes in proper education, that their children will learn from history and repeat its findings of Triumph and Victory.

Here is a letter by President George Washington, to his nephew Bushard Washington, January 15, 1783.

"Be courteous to all, but intimate with few; and let those few be well tried before you give them your confidence. True friendship is a plant of slow growth, and must undergo and withstand the shocks of adversity before it is entitled to the appellation."

I Believe

that every Child in America should learn the Classical and Majestic and Notable word called:

'Confidence'! For as a small child learns to tie his or her shoe laces and brush his or her teeth and put on their own clothes, all by themselves, and learns to sweep the floor with a tall broom; yes, this is the very early beginnings of Self- Confidence. But then the crucial moment, to where they must learn by Confidence when they are alone? This is where the Parent must lean on

Gods Almighty Trust, and believe in Gods Gracious Power to sustain the child, when he is alone or lost and or hurt. Here is where the Mom and Dad pass on the Baton of Faith to their child:

Joshua 1:9

"Have I not commanded you? Be strong and of good courage; do not be afraid, nor be dismayed, for the LORD your God is with you wherever you go."

1 Timothy 1:7

"For God has not given us a spirit of fear, but of power and of love and of a sound mind."

I Believe

in the Laws of America, for these Laws were generated from our Forefathers, for reason to protect each of us and our society as a whole. From judicial to social and to individual families; and we all know our 'Bill of Rights' and which our Founders made it very clear that we are all protected from true tyranny! So, since we are a land of public laws, do we follow them, as Loyal Patriots, or do we not follow them; as in third world countries, where every citizen does as they please, and really they don't care. Well, as an America, we do care and we all must care. Once we lose sight of our American Dream of not obeying the laws of the land; then we lose completely America the Beautiful, or the Beauty of America.

As an Illustration and a Perfect Example for you.

The Street Traffic Light:

Green means for you to move forward. **Yellow** means for you to slow down. **Red** means for you to Stop! Why? Because if you don't follow these very simple and basic Rules,… **Someone will Die!**

I Believe

in our incredible History of America, where a man named Mr. William Paca who later became a Chief Justice of the state of Maryland, then in 1782 was elected State Governor. But he was a crucial component in behalf of our freedom, for he was aware of the British Stamp Act, which they imposed upon America, without the consent of the People. And because of his fight and positive behavior as an American, his Patriotic Conduct won him favor with pushing for Independence.

And because He was for God and Country, he faced strong opposition during his tenure, but as all true Americans, adversity and trials are like 'Milk and Butter' for the Patriots.

I Believe

in Investing for our Future, especially for my family and friends, but on a global scale, being wealthy has its issues to ponder and it raises questions as to how much money does one need in life, before his or her time is up. But one must consider the consequences of where your passion and commitment is before you count your last days on earth. Here is a Story that each of us must evaluate when money is all you want?

In 1923 eight powerful money men gathered for a meeting, for their assets were more than the U.S Treasury at that time. These individuals were classified as the Financial Eagles, an Elite Group of men; and no one could achieve what they had acquired. Here is the end of each one's life:

***   Charles Schwab President:
          died penniless.

***   Richard Whitney President: served a life sentence in prison.

***   Arthor Cutton: Professional: became insolvent.

***   Albert Fall: Presidential Cabinet Member: pardoned from federal prison to die at home.

***   Jesse Livermore: Wall Street 'Bear': committed suicide.

***   Leon Fraser: President of Settlements: committed suicide.

***   Ivan Krueger: Monopoly Master: Committed suicide.

Seven of the eight extremely rich men, died in a disastrous way. Chose today, how you will spend your Valuable Time on earth, because time is Priceless.

I Believe

our Fathers in this Nation are the most influential people on the face of the earth, Mothers on the other end; are the Grand Masters of the Family. There was a Baseball player, a relief pitcher, for the Montreal Expos, New York Mets and New York Yankees. "Along with his wife, Christine, Burke adopted two orphan children from Korea, one from Vietnam, and one from Guatemala. Tim was a Born Again Christian, he retired from baseball in 1993 in order to help raise his four adopted children. And in 1994 he authored the book

Major League Dad. The moving story of an All-Star Pitcher who gave up Baseball for His Family.

Now with this story revealed to you; as a Dad, what sacrifice are you able to do, to make sure your children have a Dad; and give guidance and instruction, and most of all, the time to be with them in life, before they bloom with excitement and become great and wonderful people to help the world, just like Dad did.

I Believe

in Fathers who make an effort to be proud and honorable before they die, and what is most prestige's is that Son's are the Baton Carriers of Loyalty and Precious gold and silvers. In 1937 J.D. Rockefeller died at age 97, one of the most wealthiest persons of his time, but what is the most impressive and greatest achievement he did before his time was gone; his Son carried his deepest wishes as a true gentlemen of all of his wealth. Here is a letter from His Son, J.D. Rockefeller, Jr. wrote to his Father;

> "I have tried to do what I thought you would have me do…. I have endeavored to use wisely and unselfishly the means that you have so unselfishly placed at my disposal…. In all these years of effort and striving, your own life and example have ever been to me the most powerful and stimulating influence. What you have done for humanity and business on a vast scale has impressed me profoundly. To have been a silent partner with you in carrying out these great constructive purposes and benefactions has been the supreme delight of my life."

Here is a Bible Scripture to think upon. 1 Peter 2:21

"For to this you were called, because Christ also suffered for us, leaving us an example, that you should follow His steps.

I Believe

life is an Illustrative Process of Truth being revealed as time moves forward, for not all of the information you need growing up is given to you all at once. For it would be too much to handle!

Such as a small Finch bird, very cute and cuddly, but it can only drink so much water as you know. For a Child growing up, his mind is gathering all the information His Senses can obtain and everything is placed inside his memory; but his mind is not ready to process things that pertain to a full grown adult. That is why, tying shoelaces is a huge effort and a great accomplishment when it is done by a Five year old. So as the years drift along, and this same child reaches 18 years of age, then he is able to comprehend and gain intuition a perceptive insight into discussions of thought and intelligence. For a Wise Man, will slowly and incrementally increase prudence and discretion as time moves along, but he is careful, that the Child he is Mentoring and Coaching understands that each cornerstone is a stepping stone of mental security.

May we all , Perform patiently and diplomatically and skillfully with Wisdom, the Office of Child Rearing; as an Ambassador of Light and Life for Victory and Triumph.

Proverbs 25:11

"A word fitly spoken is like apples of gold in pictures of silver."

TRUMP PROVERBS

CHAPTER 8

I Believe

that when John F. Kennedy was assassinated, we lost a dear soul of American progress. He was a WW11 decorated Hero in 1942 during the Japan war. And he was involved with the Cold War tensions and performed honorably as he was fit to do. But during his Presidency, he gave a very interesting speech, which rings liberty bells as we speak and brings back the Pursuers of Liberty, our Founding Fathers who believed in America and the God of Heaven. Here are his precious words of wisdom to our nation, being the youngest U.S. President elected, an inaugural address, which is well-known for its powerful language and message.

January 20, 1961

"And so, my fellow Americans; ask not what your country can do for you—ask what you can do for your country. My fellow citizens of the world; ask not what America will do for you, but what together we can do for the freedom of man.

Finally, whether you are citizens of America or citizens of the world, ask of us here the same high standards of strength and sacrifice which we ask of you. With a good conscience our only sure reward, with history the final judge of our deeds, let us go forth to lead the land we love, asking His blessings and His help, but knowing that here on earth God's work must truly be our own."

I Believe

Martin Luther King was a tremendous and incredible Speaker for God, that man has ever heard. He faced incredible odds, including being rejected, for his skin was Black. The people of the world, did not realize his presence as the Presence as the God of Heaven. Hatred and Bitterness filled the air, when peace, love and humility should have been the Royal Blue Landscape. He spoke of true peace, he explained what true love was, and he lived following the Master of the Heavens. What he could not do alone, he accomplished by gathering all the Black Families of Faith to walk with him in peace. And because our world at that time, simply did not read or study the Constitution of the United States and or their Bible correctly, and did not hear the Voice of God—The Creator of the Universe; they mistakenly ignored the Love God Offers; for this kind of Love, is what Jesus and His Father shared with each other—Oh how powerful that is; … and the world missed that opportunity to experience that. And to think,…. That God Loves the Color—Black! And as a footnote, … In His Galaxies, He places all of His beautiful Stars and Planets and Meteors and Galaxies; upon a magnificent Black Drop, just to bring out the Majesty Beauty of His Creation, called His Workmanship and Masterpiece of the Heavens!

Ecclesiastes 3:11

"He hath made everything beautiful in His time; also he hath place the universe in their heart, so that no man can find out the work that God maketh from the beginning to the end."

I Believe

that whatever you pursue in life and accomplish, that reveals what kind of person you are, from intellectual to very knowledgeable, to the brilliance you have in your career, to the major contributions you have given to our Nation. But, the underlying resilience within your drive and determination and persistence ... such as the Olympic Runner who wants a Gold medal?

That inner essential and absolute essence that resides deep inside your Heart, is the Key to who you Really Are. Which means this, as they give your Eulogy at your gravesite .... Will they truthfully applaud all of your efforts and contributions and major improvements for America. Or will your departing friends, just say a few kind words and walk away.

Well, don't' Forget: next, you will face the ultimate Eulogy in front of God Almighty, and He will review your accomplishments verses His Will for your life.

Here are two verses I think you should consider as you live your life, before that great and amazing day; .... When you give up your last breath!

Matthew 6:21

"For where your treasure is, there will your heart be also."

Matthew 25:22–23

"He also that had received two talents came and said, Lord, thou delivered unto me two talents behold, I have gained two other talents beside them. His Lord said unto him, Well done, good and faithful servant; thou hast been faithful over a few things, I will make thee ruler over many things; enter thou into the joy of the Lord."

I Believe

each person who is born, leaves behind a Legacy that will contribute or take-away from Society.

And it is very unfortunate that, we are dealing with beginning children who are either directed in the right direction, or not directed and gone in the wrong direction in America! But it takes a Stand, for just One, to go against the Winds of Moral Rebellion, and not leaving behind a trail of broken and unfixable souls with marred hearts. There were two men who were both studied by different Professionals and which it began in the 1700s and they each followed their Family Tree or descendants, which still continue to this day! And what did these **descendants become**?

Father—1 Produced the following Results:

a:	1	Vice President
b:	1	Dean of Law
c:	1	Dean of Medical School
d:	3	U.S. Senators
e:	3	Governors
f:	3	Mayors
g:	13	College Presidents
h:	30	Judges
i:	60	Doctors
j:	60	Professors
k:	75	Military Officers
l:	80	Public Office Holders
m:	100	Lawyers
n:	100	Clergy
o:	285	College Graduates

Father—2 Produced the following **Results**:

a:	7	Murders
b:	60	Thieves
c:	190	Public Prostitutes
d:	150	Convicts
e:	300	Paupers
f:	440	Addition to Substance
g:	300	Died Prematurely

Who were these Men?

Father—1 was Jonathan Edwards

He was a Minister, Theologian and Missionary.

Father—2 was Max Jukes

He was an Unbeliever in God, and a man with No Principles.

I Believe

that anyone Is Able to Change **their destructive ways** and become a great and wonderful person and become productive and have a splendid career. **But it takes You to Want to Change**; it seems that for the most of us, we have to hit rock bottom and into the gutter of no return, to make a complete U-Turn. And what really happens, is that person, begins to look straight up into the Sky of Eternal Possibilities. You see, our lives are made up of Body, Soul and Spirit! Our physical part and our emotions relate to each other, and our spiritual side relates to God Alone! And once we hear Gods calling; our deepest part of our souls cries out to Him, for help! And when this happens, this is what God does for you?

The story of the Potter and the Clay, is a Classic Explanation here:

In Jeremiah 18:1–6

> "Look, as the clay is in the Potter's Hand, so are
> you in My Hand, O house of Israel."

He begins to shape and mold and design a new heart, and give you a new mind; this is what God Almighty does just for you, by simply asking Him for His divine assistance. He shows up as an Angel of Light to comfort you and hold you, right next to His Heart!

I Believe

our Children in our American society deserve to be Honored and Respected and Protected At All Cost; for they are our next generation to keep strong our Moral Values and our American Legacy! We believe in equal rights for all and complete fairness in living as an American. But there are those who want to subvert the Integrity of our Children before they grow up with true intelligence. American Children have the Right to Equal Justice under the Law, and are provided protection from those who want to harm them.

They are called Pedophiles, who hide under the wing of Educational Establishments, and implement perverted instructions in the classrooms; ... **and they have stepped into the elementary playground of children**, who are just Learning To Be Children. This movement of Sexualizing Philosophy to teach children to have sex with anything and anybody: .... is a Crime of twisted Perversion and Very Destructive. Also, including to subvert their 'Identity' and confusing them who they really are, before they are able to understand:

So here is a Warning Sign to those to Seek to Subvert our Children thru Public Education:

Jesus Christ is the Creator of the entire universe and has loan it unto us to preserve His Children and You! First of all, He says to us; before you decide to Abort your Child, ... He says, to bring them to Him first.

Matthew 19:14

"But Jesus said, Let the little children come to Me, and do not forbid them; for of such is the kingdom of heaven."

Secondly, He says, He will not play games with those to seek to hurt His Children.

Matthew 18:6

"But, whoever causes one of these little ones who believe in Me to sin, it would be better for him if a millstone were hung around his neck, and he were drowned in the depth of the sea."

I Believe

our Forefathers and Signers were not in favor of Abortion, for they were against it, and their Colonial Statutory Law and the Common Law of that day were against it. Yes, we were given rights as Americans, but the Word—Abortion, is not written in the Constitution and or Declaration of Independence. So, with that said, your rights are combined with Children's Rights! Which means that your Rights have an Honor Code of Conduct, which when an innocent child is born in the womb, or classified as Inception, …. That Child has Rights First, then the Mother has Rights after that. Here is your answer to your Rights as a Women vs your Childs Rights as a Child!

Declaration of Independence

"We hold these truths to be self-evident, that all Men are created equal, that they are endowed by their Creator with certain unalienable Rights, that among these are Life, Liberty, and the Pursuit of Happiness … etc."

Now let's hear it from the Creator Himself, as to when a Child is born:

Jeremiah 1:5

"Before I formed you in the womb I knew you;
before you were born I sanctified you; I ordained
you a prophet to the nations.:

Psalm 139:13–16

"For you formed my inward parts, you knitted me together in my
mother's womb. I praise you for I am fearfully and wonderfully
made. Wonderful are your works; my soul knows it very well.
My frame was not hidden from you when I was being made
in secret, intricately woven in the depths of the earth."

I Believe

the Greatest Leader in the entire world was and still is Jesus Christ! He in
His Book of Life, says that He created the entire Universe, with all of its
Galaxies, and which the Milky Way Galaxy is where we live in. Our planet
the Earth is suspended in space and rotating around the Sun and at the
same time our Earth spins on its axis at a speed of 1,000 miles per hour.
He not only is a Personal Leader and a National Leader, He is our Chief
architect of Planets and keeps everything from colliding into each other by
using his Beautiful 'Gravity' System; which keeps us glued to the earth and
the planets around the Earth, don't collided out of control, because of **His
Universal Leadership.**

Every Galaxy obeys His divine wishes, and so should we! Everything on
Earth is perfect for Humanity to live in, and it is perfect in harmony with
Physics and Masterful geometry and including the electrical mechanical
field around the Earth and the Ozone Layer as our Shield of Protection

from universe dust and particles. So, who is our Leader on Earth, not any of us, for He has called us to do only One Thing on Earth; **and that is to Follow Him, and Obey His simple Commands of**: To Love Him with all of our Hearts and Minds and Soul, and to Love each other as ourselves. So, if Love is the Essential Equation and the Divine Requirement; … then this is a No Brainer! Love is the Answer!

I Believe

a Father and Son relationship is a Historical Tradition that has established the strength and stability and sound dignity for honoring a Father and a Son. Rest assured, without this Bond in America, we would have never been a country and or a Nation. **The magnificence and majestic value of this relationship,** is how a Family begins to grow into a Masterpiece of Family Poetry.

Where stories and time create a beautiful Mosaic of Memories. This amazing and remarkable experience, is forever a tapestry of joy, as a fabric of royalty, given to a King as a Gift of Gratitude.

Now here is a Story!

'There was man who joined the military and served in the Canadian Air Force in 1942 and later the Army Air Core. And by his efforts and determination to serve our country well, he obtained a Silver Star and became a War Hero.

And by his 'Example as a Patriot,' his Son took notice. So he enlisted and was commissioned into the Officer Training School; but before he finished, within 1 week before graduation, he was denied. He was to be dismissed due to a health ailment. He was devastated and his life seemed to end, for He wanted to follow his Father's footsteps.

So, he contacted his Father and explained his sad Story, ... And his Father, contacted a leading General at the time, and explained the current problem about his son. The discussion was never made known, but his Son, was able to continue and Graduate as Second Lieutenant. Then a Military Miracle took place, for before his Son retired, he was able to implement the U.S. Space Command, which later called, 'Space Force'. He Built the Reorganizational Proposal for the review at the Pentagon, and because of his efforts and his team; it was approved and accepted. So you see, this is how the Almighty God of America works, to make it strong and mighty as our Forefathers did. And by the way, his name is—Classified!

But we call him…The Big Cheese!

I Believe

that America is Great because of God Given people decided to live for Him; and which no man or woman is perfect in anyway, for we all need daily His Love and Grace and Food to survive while living on Earth. But, while in the process of America being made great, France took notice;

For in 1865, a French political intellectual and anti- slavery activist named Edouard de Laboulaye proposed that a Statue Representing Liberty be built for the United States.

This monument would Honor the United States Centennial of Independence and the Friendship with France. The Citizens of France gave this as a Gift to the Citizens of America, to celebrate the liberty of the world. The Statute of Liberty!

So far, as a Nation of Liberty and Freedom; … why hasn't any other Nation contributed to us thus far—under the Biden Administration?

I Believe

United States of America is a Nation that has been Chosen by God Himself, as a nation blessed with liberty. As we follow our history back to the Founding Fathers, and how they were brought together; for such a time as this! Our Nation is a Country that God was asked for His assistance in guiding and protecting our heritage, such as the American Flag was erected as our National Symbol. But, what holds America above all other nations around us, and why do every country in the whole world want their children to be educated on U.S. Soil? What makes the difference, is that America is filled with Churches of the Christian Faith and we are a Nation of Prayer and God hears our request! Just consider, how many wars America has gone through, and what were the reasons? They were to help the weak of the world, because tyranny enemies were so abusive and evil, such as the Communist Party; that America could not just set by and watch them get slaughtered. God has been honored for our courage and human effort to protect His People!

Proverbs 14:34

  "Righteousness exalts a nation, but sin is a reproach to any people."

I Believe

the Scientist Isaac Newton, used the Thumb Print as Evidence of the Existence of God, because each person has an individual and unique thumb print.

  "He argued that this pointed to a Designer rather than random chance."

  "In the absence of any other proof, the thumb alone would convince me of God's existence. And he also said, "The Supreme God is a Being eternal, infinite, and absolutely perfect. Opposition to godliness is atheism in profession and idolatry in practice. Atheism is so senseless and odious to mankind that it never had many professors."

And by comparison, he was ten times smarter than Albert Einstein, because Iascc Newton believe that God was the all Creator of the Universe and Mankind.

Genesis 1:1

"In the beginning God created the heavens and the earth."

It is rather interesting, that the Hebrew word for Created is: "bara", which means, out of nothing He Created the Heavens and the Earth. He actually spoke it ... into Existence.

I Believe

when the Declaration of Independence was being drafted and deliberated on, that many statesmen and distinguished diplomats contributed their best to make a magna carta of balance; and which when it was completely finished and penned, God was mentioned three times in the written presentation.

And for the beautiful Constitution of the United States, our Forefathers made sure, that no one was to be forced to Believe in one state religion as such; but they wanted us to Believe Willingly, because the God of the Universe is a God of Love. And if you or I don't love someone, then we are able to walk away and not believe.

"Congress shall make no law respecting an establishment of religion, or prohibiting the free exercise thereof; or abridging the freedom of speech, or of the press; or the right of the people peaceably to assemble, and to petition the Government for a redress of grievances."

So, as Americans, our Forefathers knew in advance what the next generation of children needed to hear from their voices who guided them to establish the Freedom Papers of Glory!

Psalm 19:7–9

"The law of the LORD is perfect, converting the soul; the testimony of the LORD is sure, making wise the simple. The statutes of the LORD are right, rejoicing the heart; the commandment of the LORD is pure, enlightening the eyes. The fear of the LORD is clean, enduring forever; the judgements of the LORD are true and righteous altogether."

I Believe

our lives are not our own, for we never know when our time is up, and when it happens, we are struck by illness or a quick defeat of death. Such as Thomas Lynch Jr. born in South Carolina.

His father Thomas Lynch Sr., gave up his wealth for the commitment of independence and was respected of the Second Continental Congress; for which he influence the appointment of George Washington as Commander-in-Chief of the Continental Army. He convinced the New England delegation through John Adams and then convinced the Southern delegation, **and the career of Washington began**. Then Thomas Lynch Sr, suffered a second stroke and died and his son Thomas Lynch jr. also suffered a serious disease that almost took his life, when he was Captain of the South Carolina Regiment. And what is so wonderful here, is that his son took his place in Congress, and became a Signer of the Declaration of Independence.

Psalm 90:12

"Teach us to number our days and recognize how few they are; help us to spend them as we should."

I Believe

in Sacred Matrimony under the tender guidance of the Almighty, the Creator of the Universe, who has given each star a name and has made every snow flake completely unlike each other, and for every grain of sand upon the Earths surface; that is how many times He thinks of you and me!

As a Man vows to love his wife, and as a Woman vows to love her husband; … then with both vows coming together, then there is a Consecrated Promise Made as One. This means placing your Promise inside a Vault of Love and it is sealed, till death do you part! But in today's world of people not willing to Walk side by side with Him; they decide without His Advice or Wise Counsel and break off the Marriage. So, whoever is at fault, in troubling the pure fresh springs of Marriage, is the one who needs to Repent and say, I am Sorry!

Why, because God who Created you: "Hates Divorce!'

For it fractures and breaks the tender hearts that we carry; in fact, we were never designed for divorce. Our five senses and our entire heart, body and soul, become dismantled. Love is our healing balm and gentle ointment of forgiveness and restoration. We all know what God wants for each of us; He wants us to be won over by His divine Compassion and His eternal loving kindness. And God knows, we are not perfect people.

Mark 10:6–9

'But from the beginning of the creation, God made them male and female. For this cause shall a man leave his father and mother, and cleave to his wife; And they twain shall be one flesh; so, then they are no more twain, but one flesh. What therefore God hath joined together, let not man put asunder."

I Believe

that Education was a genuine goldmine for our Forefathers and for our Fathers of today. But because of our enemies who are merely of Communist nature; Fathers must be on guard to protect our Country from this ideology an atheistic behavior, that aims to denounce the God of the Universe. God has given His people Intelligence and knowledge worthy of thought; to build up America and to keep it strong for the next generation to come. For without healthy intelligence, America will cease to exist, as a Leading Supreme Power.

Here is a letter from President John Adams, to Abigail Adams May 12, 1780.

"I must study politics and war, that my sons may have the liberty to study mathematics and philosophy, geography, natural history, and naval architecture, navigation, commerce, and agriculture, in order to give their children a right to study painting, poetry, music, architecture, statuary, tapestry and porcelain."

I Believe

our beloved President Abraham Lincoln, had a great and wonderful Prayer Life.

"Bless our land with honorable ministry, sound learning, and pure manners. Save us from violence, discord, and confusion, from pride and arrogance, and from every evil way. Defend our liberties, and fashion into one united people, the multitude brought hither out of many kindreds and tongues."

After 3 months after his assassination, a writer named Noah Brooks reported that Abraham Lincoln once said:

"I have been driven many times upon my knees by the overwhelming conviction that I had no where else to go. My own wisdom and that of all about me seem insufficient for that day."

I Believe

we must be Open-Minded for the Future of our Country called America, we should continually be aware of our Values and our Habits as a people who want to be the Greatest Nation on Earth. For if we choose, not to be the greatest Nation on Earth; then, we will fall under the dictatorship of someone. And let us not forget Hitler, who was an atheist and a hater of America, and killed anyone who was not a Marxist and a Communist!

Just glean at his track record, in how he ran his country, and in fact, look at China with all of their Concentrations Camps for old, young and children who do not fit their elite plan of Communism.

Today, in the world, America is either loved or hated; and You Have To Choose one or the other. For if you only focus on Equal Rights and not Building up America as our Founding Fathers did and Sacrifice their entire lives and welfare, for Freedom and Liberty and Freedom to Worship and

Prosperity; **then you should move to China** and live in their camps, because it shows, **you are Lazy and Pathetic and Visionless**.

For to be an American and live on Sacred land, who's Blood was shed for our Freedom; … Our Sons and Daughters to this day; they have Proven to be Worthy of Honor and Praise… as they lay on Sacred Ground—The Cemetery of the Fallen!

I Believe

our Country, the United States of America, **is in a serious crises of survival**, for our top money power brokers who are billionaire's, have reaped the benefits of the American Democracy, and are not contributing to our Constitution and Declaration of Independence, which made America Great! Their prosperity is being used against us, as a People who Believe in Freedom.

They Choose to 'Steal' Power by Force over the People, that we may be subject to their Rulership.

In Congress, there is a Nasty and Crude group of people, who focus only in destroying our Democracy; by breaking every law and trying to implement laws that gives and makes them Powerful at the Top. While the little people who work for a living, are paying their salary and they are taking our money, and giving it to tyrants around the world who want to destroy America. These people Will Be Judge fairly, and here is Paul the Apostle on this subject.

Romans 12:19

"Beloved, do not avenge yourselves, but rather give place to wrath; for it is written, "Vengeance is Mine, I will repay," says the Lord."

I Believe

we should Be a Passionate People of America, who press forward with Vision and Courage, and Always Be an Example of Excellence!

> "We the People who we should Be, We the People
> who should be, We the People are to be!"

I Believe

… America Belongs to God, and Not Us!!! We were placed here to do His Wishes and Dreams, not ours. What is His Wish? For You to Belong to Him. As a Gift that he can hold and cherish and adore—Forever!

And what is His Dream?

That you would live with Him, … for Eternity; and what is so simple here, is that you would Walk and Talk to Him each and every day.

For He has placed His Creation before you, to prove to You, that He is the Almighty God and there is none else. For He is Proud of you every day, because You are His. You say, "Not Me"

Oh Yes You. Because remember, that He is a Father, and You are His Child. And He knows what you need before you ask Him. Why?

Because He adores You and Loves You! What is so amazing and incredible, is that He Thought of You, before you were born. So, His plans for you have been on the drawing board for a long time, for you to have fun, with Him, your Maker and Your Father.

Psalm 19:1–3

"The heavens declare the glory of God; and the firmament shows His handiwork. Day unto day utters speech, and night unto night reveals knowledge. There is no speech nor language where their voice is not heard. Their line has gone out through all the earth, and their words to the end of the world. In them He has set a tabernacle for the sun."

Ephesians 1:4–5

"Just as He chose us in Him before the foundation of the world, that we should be holy and without blame before Him in love. Having predestined us to adoption as sons by Jesus Christ to Himself, according to the good pleasure of His will."

I Believe

today in America, by what we see happening here with riots and protest and burning the American Flag, and murders and rapes and child abuse and kidnappings and sex trafficking and an outburst of pornography on the web and divorce and wars and other countries who are communist and the haters of America, such as the Hamas regime and genocide against Americas, and China forcing drug trade to our cartels and then killing our children, and pedophiles pushing to indoctrinate our children into homosexuality, and including our Open Boarders with no common sense; where children and young people being raped and tagged for money from the cartels just to pass into United States. And the majority trying to cross, are dying in the process by drowning and having no food or water.

The question you have to ask is;

"Why Is This Happening?"

Our Founding Fathers fought for our Country to be Free from tyranny, and they were all God Fearing People who cared for each other graciously. But see, our Founding Fathers knew that they had to live a good life and please God Almighty in order for Him to Bless this Nation.

Well, compare them to us today

We are not listening to Him and we are not Obeying His very simple commands; …to Love one another as He Loves You.

Here is a Bible verse that Paul the Apostle gave us to consider for our sake:

Galatians 6:7

> "Do not be deceived, God is not mocked;
> for whatever a man sows, that he will also reap."

I Believe

everybody who is born in America, is called to Greatness for America. Greatness is an Attitude! It is a God Given Talent to everyone…

A hidden secret inside every heart, that has been placed there by the God of the Universe. Look in our history from our Founding Fathers all the way to here now; …. All of the Scientist, Chemist, Mathmagicians. Doctors, Nurses, Val Victorians, Silver Stars, Medal of Honors, Purple Hearts and our Volunteers and Christian Missionaries into all of the World to share the Love of Jesus Christ!

But you say; 'I can't do this alone, and I just don't know how?"

Well, my answer to You my Friend, is You have the 'Signature of God" upon your life! You carry His Image and Likeness, for He favors you, as you are. He will come along side you and guide you into His Greatness.

A Greatness no one can take away.

Just imagine the Bumble Bee, how strong it is and how powerful it is and how magnificent it is, and what it does for the entire world. For this same greatness is and has been placed inside your Heart. Did you know? That Bee's to produce a pound of Honey, … one Bee must visit 2 million flowers and collect its wonderful nectar, and in the process of its effort and dedication and commitment and loyalty and joy of its Quest for Greatness. It must travel 90 thousand miles, or 3 times around the entire world globe…. To produce 1 pound of Sweet Honey!

So, if an Amazing Bee can do all of this, and it was designed and created by Your Father in Heaven; **what do you think He can do with You?**

I Believe

our Mothers of America, are tremendous people who lead and guide their children in a Beautiful Way! For after they give birth to a cute and tiny child, the Mothers Love just grows like a Sequia Tree, and reaches beyond boundaries a potential that she gives to her child and children. A Mothers Love is so profound and magnificent and brilliantly designed, that the child she is raising up to be Special and Great, … ends up with Her Signature of being Splendid and Majestic.

Children have a resemblance of Angels and that is placed there from God Himself! Just as the Rainbow in the sky after a storm, or just as the Northern Lights of Beauty, and or the billions upon billions of Stars in the twilight, camping upon the mountains such as Yosemite National Park. For The Love of a Mother imitates the Creator she serves, and He promises to help her, as under the Wings of an Eagle, which flies higher than any bird known to mankind.

I Believe

the Faith of a Mother, or any Mother, is a powerful instrument in the time of trouble or severe crises.

There was a time of a Mother who wanted her child to reach her dreams, and she ask God for help, she wasn't sure how He was going to do it; but her Faith in God Almighty, who created the entire universe; she trusted in that. So, when her daughter who wanted to become a concert singer, was denied entrance to a famous music conservatory, on the account of her race and her skin Black; her Mother just said: "Someone would be raised up to Help."

Well, as she Prayed to God her Father, who she believed was a Promise Keeper, she just waited upon Him.

Well, in the city of Philadelphia, an outstanding voice teacher, named Mr. Giuseppe Boghetti, made room for her to become one of his students. Her Mother knew, God would pull them through, for within time; her little daughter who wanted to sing her heart for America, got her chance. For in 1939 on Easter Sunday, she sang for more than 75 thousand people gathered in front of the Lincoln Memorial, and to this day, has never been forgotten.

And who is this Sweet Lady we have been talking about; well, her name is "Marian Anderson."

Who sang for both inaugurations of Dwight D., Eisenhower and John F. Kennedy and was a recipient of the Presidential Medal of Freedom?

And by chance, guess who was able to attend this beautiful concert, at the age of 10 years old. None other than, Martin Luther King. So, you see how God Works through lives of His People, who Believe in Him.

A THOUGHT TO PONDER

What do you **Believe In**, and what do you do to continue in what you believe in.

This thought process will explain where you are at on American soil, as an American, or as an Enemy of America.

What lives and dwells in the **Center of your Heart**, determines your future.

What you Invest Inside Your Heart, will either create a Masterful Plan for You and Others, or you will create Death and Destruction.

Question: What do You Believe in?

Our Founding Fathers,

Believed in the Almighty and His Wishes and Dreams for our Country. They put into practice a Belief System, including the Majesty Maker of the Universe, and from Him they obtained the most Beautiful Words of Wisdom mankind could have ever had.

From their **Belief System**, we have received the most comprehensive and remarkable transcripts any country could have ever obtained: The True Directives from Heaven's Door.

The Constitution of the United States of America

And

The Declaration of Independence

NOTE FROM THE AUTHOR

May you be fully Blessed from the God of the Universe, for without Him you will perish and die without light and hope.

Our Founding Fathers, begged and Prayed and wished that all Believers in their post treaties of the American Dream; …. **Would be Followed!**

They were Inspired in their Heart, by God alone!

For without their Passion and Dedication and Effort and Inner Hope to be a Free Nation…

The City on the Hill, would have never come True!

They did deliberate and fight amongst themselves, in what to do and in what to say and in how to say; and it took them time of Prayer to develop and voted in favor of our Countries Most Beautiful Work of Poetic Art Words of Freedom.

For as the Universe continues to Shine in the twilight of the night; for it Never Fails to Disappoint Us, so, Let Us Also Shine and Never Disappoint our Country; **The United States of America**

Books By: Richard Delgado

Art Proverbs a Masterpiece
Marriage Proverbs for Christmas
Leadership Proverbs for Corporate America
Trump Proverbs A Man After Gods Own Heart

We Offer: American Leadership Training Classes

1. **American Principles**
2. **Our Founding Fathers Passion**
3. **You Are Chosen To Lead**
4. **What Makes America Great**

Note: This is a 6 to 8 Hour Session. With our Team of Instructors.

For Classes of groups of 25 to 100. We come to your Corporation: **There is a Corporate Cost.**

Contact: Mr. Darren Melugin
Email: info@leadyou.org

We will Provide you with a Returned Email, with a Basic Outline of our Sessions of Training.

Then upon Agreement of Schedule and Time.

Our Team Leader will make Final Arrangements with your Corporation, and answer any questions you may have.

www.ingramcontent.com/pod-product-compliance
Lightning Source LLC
Chambersburg PA
CBHW022101020426
42335CB00012B/774